Love,
Lashes,
and
Lipstick

Love, Lashes, and Lipstick

My Secrets for a Gorgeous, Happy Life

mally roncal

Illustrations by Alisa Chompupong

BALLANTINE BOOKS ‚ NEW YORK

Published in the United States by Ballantine Books, an imprint of Random House, a division of Random House LLC, a Penguin Random House Company, New York.

BALLANTINE and the HOUSE colophon are registered trademarks of Random House LLC.

The photos on pages 118, 121, 144, and 145 courtesy of Getty Images. The bottom left photo on page 124 is courtesy of Adrian Vecchio, Kismet Photography. The photos on pages ii, viii, 82–83, 87, 101, 124 (top center; top right; second row, left; second row, right; third row, left), 125 (third row, left; bottom row, second from left), 128, 130, 132–33, 138, 152, 153, 154, 156 (top three photos), 157, 180, 187, and 199 are courtesy of Phil Bickett. All others are courtesy of Mally Roncal.

Library of Congress Cataloging-in-Publication Data
Roncal, Mally
Love, lashes, and lipstick : my secrets for a gorgeous, happy life /
Mally Roncal.
pages cm
ISBN 978-0-8041-7823-5
eBook ISBN 978-0-8041-7824-2
1. Makeup artists—United States—Biography. 2. Cosmetics. 3. Beauty, Personal. 4. Celebrities—Miscellanea. I. Title.
[DNLM: 1. Roncal, Mally.]
TT955.R66A3 2014
646.7'2092—dc23 [B]   2014025969

Printed in the United States of America on acid-free paper

www.ballantinebooks.com

9 8 7 6 5 4 3 2 1

First Edition

Book design by Liz Cosgrove

To my incredible husband Phil—there are almost no words in the English language to express what you are to me. You are my partner in life, love, parenthood, and business. You are my best friend, my rock, my coach, my teacher, my soul, and the best daddy on the planet. You inspire me more than anyone in the world, and without you I would not be the woman I am today. There's nothing we can't do together!

To my three beautiful babies, Pilar, Sophie, and Vivienne. Every breath I take is only for your sake. You're funny, smart, kind, respectful, and sweet. Your light and joy truly show me the face of God. You make me want to be a better person every single day and there is nothing on earth I love more than being your mommy.

I love you all the mostest!

Contents

Introduction:
The Phones Are on Fire!

T'S MARCH 5, 2005, AND I AM READY. AS A LONGTIME QVC WATCHER and customer (I remember being lulled to sleep by the channel on the TV in my bedroom as a child), this day is my dream come true.

My makeup line, Mally Beauty, is launching with a one-hour show on a Saturday in a prime-time afternoon spot. The host who had been assigned to our show, Jill Bauer, is pregnant and was put on mandatory bed rest yesterday. Her replacement, Patti Reilly, stayed on the phone with me for two hours on Friday night so I could teach her everything about our line and products. When I finally got off the phone with her, I felt confident that she would do a great job. I'm excited!

Last night, my husband, Phil, our team, and I had a little party in the hotel room. We knew we hadn't sold one single product yet, but I felt strongly about celebrating the fact that we were actually there! I looked at Phil and asked him, "Can you believe how far we've come?"

This morning we got up at the butt crack of dawn. There are no words to describe how I feel—somewhere between a pure adrenaline rush, giddy excitement, and diarrhea. I just want to get there and do it!

We get to Studio Park, Pennsylvania, headquarters for QVC, promptly at 10:00 A.M. Phil, my assistant Teenie, our two makeup artists, and all of our models get to work: The show won't start until one, but we have *hours* of prep. Models' "before" shots have to be taken; makeup has to be done; *my* hair and makeup have to be done; we have to meet with our producers; set dressers have to arrange the products; and everything has to be PER*FOIS*. Everyone who is important to me is there in the green room: Phil, my dad and stepmom, my cousins, and all our buyers. We have brought dozens of yellow roses, my late mother's favorite flowers, to put on the set.

I'll be selling the six products that have defined my signature look as a celebrity makeup artist: Cancellation Concealer, the first truly bulletproof brightening concealer; Visible Skin Foundation, the fastest, easiest way to get a perfect complexion; Shimmer, Shape, and Glow (which I say gives you the look of a face-lift, as if you just lost five pounds and had sex with Channing Tatum); Lightwand Eye Brightener (a.k.a. eight hours of sleep in a pen); as well as my Smokey Eye Kit and Life, Love, and a Really Great Lipgloss, neither of which needs an explanation.

Showtime!

I put on the gorgois pink velvet Marc Jacobs suit I bought specifically for this occasion, slip into my high heels, and walk to the studio operations room, where they give me an earpiece (which doesn't fit very well), wire me for sound, and make sure that I am on the same frequency as my host and everyone else on the show, so we'll all be hearing the same thing. Then someone says, "Are you excited?" and I say, "Oh, yeah," and, holding hands with Phil and my team, say a little prayer. I hear someone say, "Good luck," then I take a deep breath and walk out on set. I've spent months preparing for this moment, and failure is not an option.

There I stand, behind a table with my products right in front of me, my host to my left and a model between us. My heart is pounding a mile a minute and I have to remember to breathe. At QVC, everything is done remotely; all you see are cameras with numbers on them and red lights on top. I hear a voice in my ear:

"Hi, Mally, this is Joe from the control room. How are you feeling? Give me a thumbs-up. . . . Okay, great. We can see everything's fine; you just do your thing. When you see the red light lit up, the camera's on; that's where you look." Got it!

> **"Mally, they love it! The phones are on fire!"**

There are two screens on the floor in front of me. One shows a live shot—that's what the world is seeing right now; the other screen is the next shot up. If screen number one is showing me, the host, and the model talking, and screen number two is a close-up of the model's face, then I need to get ready to demo. It's like patting your head and rubbing your belly at the same time: You've got to stay in the moment, get ready for the next shot, listen to what the voice in your ear is saying, talk to your host, and pretend that none of this is happening. Easy, right?

Off to the side I see Teenie, clipboard in hand, directing my makeup artists as they finish touching up the models. The voice in my ear asks, "Mally, you're all set?" The light goes on and here we go. There's no turning back on live TV; it's like the Olympics. You hit it, or you don't.

Patti introduces me, and I think I'm going to be nervous, but I'm not. I feel completely at home, chatting with and teaching my new best friends. At the same time I'm thinking, *Oh, God, I hope it goes right. Okay, what model is that? Is she supposed to be sitting there?* It's just a whirlwind of activity and information, and then the voice in my ear says, "Mally, they love it! The phones are on fire!"

When you're on air, "the phones are on fire" is what you live for. Somewhere in a room, someone is sitting in front of a computer screen that shows the call volume. A steady line means sales are okay. When a product is really working, you get a spike in calls, and then it usually goes back down. When the phones are on fire, whatever you're presenting is going, going, GONE!

The voice says, "Keep doing what you're doing, girl, they love it. . . . Okay, you're about to sell out, it's going to sell out!" And I'm talking about the next product and trying not to react, because you don't say, "Oh my God, we're selling out!" on air.

THAT WAS THE MOST amazing, exhilarating day of my life. We sold out every item. It was supposed to be an hour-long show, and we had nothing left after forty-five minutes. It was a record; no beauty brand had ever done that before.

I was dancing and singing in the car all the way back home to New York. It was magical. I knew our lives had changed that day. It was as if the seas had parted; the world had opened up and was ours for the taking. That was when I knew—no matter how big or impossible it seemed—that if you can believe it, then it can happen.

Every day, life shows us little lessons and miracles. You just have to keep your eyes open to see them. I mean, let's be honest, sometimes life sucks. Everything doesn't always go your way. But if you look really deep into any situation, there is almost always something to learn, and you can use those experiences to your advantage, to grow.

In this book, I am going to share with you stories—some funny, some embarrassing, some sweet, some sad—and some of the many lessons I've learned in my life. I'm also going to share tips, tricks, and makeup techniques I've used on my celebrity clients and other beautiful women, like you, to make them look as gorgois on the outside as they are on the inside.* Because beauty isn't just about mascara and concealer; it's about who we are and how we see ourselves. I find beauty in everything and everyone, and I want you to be able to do that too.

So, my loves, are you ready to look and feel your most gorgois ever?

Then let's go!

---

* You can duplicate these looks with your favorite go-to colors and brands, but if you want to know which Mally Beauty products to use, turn to page 205.

Love,
Lashes,
and
Lipstick

chapter

1

My Chanel Training Heels

MY MOM CALLED ME HER MIRACLE BABY. DOCTORS HAD told her she couldn't have a child, but one day she woke up and said to my father, "I'm pregnant." He didn't believe her, but here I am, proof that she was right. As usual.

Mommy was fabulous in every way. She was an ob-gyn who had delivered more than one thousand babies over her career and was the director of the Medical/Surgical Unit at the Middletown Psychiatric Center in New York. She wore designer clothes under her white doctor's coat and the highest heels to the office. And she never went out without her "face" on.

Just before I turned one, Mommy was diagnosed with breast cancer. Her doctors gave her six months to live.

Just after my mom was diagnosed. I'm almost one year old.

She knew we were not going to have a lot of time together, and I understand now that she vowed not to go anywhere until she was sure I would be okay on my own. Even with this disease hanging over our heads like a dark cloud, she lived as if the sun was shining bright every day, and we made more memories in the too-few years we had together than most people do in a hundred. To say we were close is an understatement; our bond was indescribable. As far back as I can remember, she did all she could, all the time, to make sure I would be ready for what life was going to throw at me, even if we did some things just a *little* early. She wanted me to be prepared for *anything*.

"Always wear your Lipstick!" "Okay, Mommy, but I'm like ten years old!"

I can still hear her pronouncements—born in the Philippines, she never quite conquered the V's and F's of English, except when she said "love."

Whenever I left the house:

"Always wear your lipstick!"

"Okay, Mommy, but I'm like ten years old!"

"What*eber,* Melissa! That's no excuse!" (And, yes, I always wear lipstick when I go out!)

Whenever I met a boy that I liked:

"Ip a boy likes you, he will call you. You won't hab to call him." (Call me old-fashioned, but that's what I believe to this day. And when it's the right time, I will tell my girls the same thing.)

Whenever I met someone new:

"Always look them in the eye. Shake their hand pirmly and remember their name. And call them by it!" (And I do. Every time.)

Whenever I lost weight:

"Take your clothes to the tailor and hab them pitted. That way, there is no room to gain weight again!" (We *both* did that. And ended up having to buy new clothes. I don't go to the tailor as often now. I have "fat" jeans *and* "skinny" jeans.)

On why I had so many "uncles" and no aunts:

"Don't worry about it, honey. Love is the same eberywhere and with eberyone."

Drills in heels—just a *wee* bit early

And one of my favorites:

"Always work hard, be humble, pray to God, and have pun in everything that you do. Lipe is too sweet and too precious to waste. Honor God in ebery moment of your existence." (And, yes, I do this. Every single day.)

Then there was the day that she called me into her room and said:

"Honey, I hab to break the news to you. You are neber going to grow ober pibe peet tall. [Translation: You are never going to grow over five feet tall.] I want you to put on these Chanel heels and practice running up and down the stairs."

Really? I was in the fourth grade.

But, sure enough, while all the other kids were outside playing, I was hut-hutting it up and down two flights in black pumps with four-inch heels. I might have thought it was a little crazy, but, to be honest, I loved it too. And you know what? Today I can walk in heels the way other women walk in ballet flats.

And, for the record, I'm five one and three-quarters.

MY MOM WAS ALWAYS passionate about doing what she wanted *today*. Not knowing exactly how long she had to live made her live every single day as if it were her last. Because she never wanted to miss a moment with me, her miracle baby, I was always a part

The day before, we were in Middletown, New York.

of her little adventures. There was the time that she decided, "Let's go to Europe," and the next day we were all on a plane to Paris.

Or the time she crept into my room at the butt crack of dawn and whispered, "Melissa! Let's go out bepore Daddy wakes up! We'll go to Cartier and buy all our priends watches!" (We ended up at Louis Vuitton and got everyone purses.)

"We should go to Saks and get you a makeover!"

Then there was the day that changed the direction of my life—the day my obsession with makeup began.

"*Anak* [*anak* means 'my child' in Tagalog, one of the official languages of the Philippines], I was thinking that maybe we should go to Saks and get you a makeober!"

A makeover? I was in sixth grade!

"You're old enoup now that you should be wearing makeup! Let's habe someone teach you how! We'll have pun!"

Now, do I think twelve-year-olds should be wearing a full face of makeup? No. When my girls start wearing makeup, it will be some lip gloss and mascara when they're in eighth grade. But Mommy didn't want to miss out on this rite of passage for a mother and daughter.

We ended up sitting on the stools at the Elizabeth Arden counter at Saks Fifth Avenue in New York City. A handsome, very fabulous, very made-up man came over to us.

"Helllllllooooo, dahlings!!!! Well, aren't you gorgeous? What can I do for you today? Do we need a little something?"

Mommy and I beamed at him. He was fierceness personified!

"Yes, my love," Mommy said. "This is my daughter, Melissa. She needs a makeober. Can you teach us how to give her the perfect face she needs?"

"Well, of course, dahlings! This is what I'm here for!"

He stood back, put his hand under my chin, and turned my face from side to side, studying it, then went to work. I can only describe what happened next as a whirlwind of deliciousness. His fingers were flying like Edward Scissorhands's as powders and creams and brushes came at me from every direction. The scent of Eight Hour Cream filled the air, and even now when I smell it I remember that day. Mommy just smiled and smiled. I was in heaven. There was something about being surrounded by all the products and brushes and the hustle and bustle and perfumes of the cosmetics floor. I watched him carefully considering his choices as he selected the colors to apply to my face. I so envied his creativity. I knew that someday I wanted to be able to touch people the way he did.

When Mr. Fabulous Makeup Artist was through, he stood back and admired his work: foundation, powder, purple and pink eye shadow, black eyeliner, mascara, hot-pink blush, candy-pink lipstick—the works. (Remember, this was the early eighties.) I looked at Mommy; she had tears of happiness in her eyes.

Snuck in a little bit of Elizabeth Arden stash, just for the pic!

"She's perpect! We'll take it all!"

Best. Day. Ever.

Mommy was preparing me. Teaching me. She understood that every moment is precious, and by living in the moment she was getting me ready for the future, her way, with the things that mattered to her. Of course, it wasn't just about clothes or high heels or boys. It was about life and kindness, work ethic and faith. It's not always easy—in fact, it's impossible—to be prepared for everything, but you can do your best to be ready for any situation, any issue, big or little.

Skin Care How-To

One of the most important beauty lessons my mom taught me was how to take care of my skin. Of course, we both spent too many hours baking in the sun, coated in Hawaiian Tropic suntan oil, SPF zero. Who knew that the beautiful golden tan I had at sixteen meant sun spots when I was forty? Here are two simple but effective skin-care routines that will work for you, regardless of your age or your (past!) bad habits.

Skin Care A.M.

1. Okay, this may sound cray cray, but do not wash your face in the morning. Nighttime is when your skin regenerates and repairs itself, so washing in the morning undoes all those benefits and can dry you out. Just splash on a little warm water and pat your face dry (that's what I do), or, if you must (but you really shouldn't need to if you cleanse your face properly before you go to bed), use a very mild moisturizing cleanser.

2. If you're using a serum, now's the time to apply it. Use one that addresses your skin-care concerns, whether it's dryness, brightening, oil control, or anti-aging.

3. Apply a moisturizer with SPF. Every day. Especially if you're using a retinol product at night. If it's raining, snowing, cloudy—even if you don't go outside. And don't forget your neck (front and back), chest, and ears! If you use a moisturizer *and* a sun protection product, use your SPF first.

4. Tap on a little eye cream under your eye, using your ring finger (it has the lightest touch). You don't need more than a pea-sized amount for both eyes.

5. Apply makeup primer to seal in all your skin-care goodness and prepare your face for makeup.

6. Smooth on some lip balm.

Skin Care P.M.

1. The most important thing you can do for your skin is to CLEANSE. I cannot stress this enough! No matter what time it is or how tired I am, I never go to bed with makeup on my skin. EVER. It's my most important beauty rule, and I never break it.

2. Apply eye cream. The skin around your eyes is one of the first places to show signs of aging.

3. Follow with a moisturizer. If you want serious anti-aging action, look for something containing retinol, a derivative of Vitamin A proven to even out skin tone and to smooth wrinkles.

4. Don't forget a neck cream. Like your eyes, your neck shows signs of aging quickly.

5. Don't forget lip balm.

MORE IS MORE

You know how everyone is always talking about "Less is more"? Well, that may be true of some things: sugar in your coffee, powder on your face, self-tanner.

But for me, not so much. At least not when it comes to life. Maybe it's because we never knew exactly when my mother's last day was going to be. So you know what? We chose "more." My assistant Gabrielle once said, "You like to take every single minute of the day and suck every single second out of it!" (I promise, she meant it in a good way!) And it's true. We have so few minutes in this life. Suck them dry. Make the most out of them. Take a spontaneous trip to the park with your kids. Run after the ice cream truck. Treat yourself to a pedicure. Carve out an hour for exercise class, and even if you detest it and you're crying through those leg lifts, get what you came for. Throw a luau-themed party in the middle of October (grass skirts, coconuts, and all) for no reason other than it's Tuesday. Say *yes.* And if that just means chillin' in front of your TV and eating popcorn one day, no problem! Do it with passion and love, every single second of it.

Take a moment. Take the time!

Tuesday afternoon luau

chapter

2

Treat Everyone Like a Superstar

I F I HAD TO CHOOSE THE MOST IMPORTANT lesson my parents taught me, it was that everyone wants to be heard, deserves to be heard, and should be treated with love and respect. When I was a little girl, I would go to work with them (my dad, a psychiatrist, worked at the same hospital as my mom) and be inspired—and I'm still inspired—not just by their commitment to healing people's minds and bodies but also by seeing the way that they treated people. Their kindness and dedication to making people feel good about themselves made me love them even more, and I always try to emulate them.

My parents always knew and acknowledged the inner and outer beauty in everyone, and they passed that to me. Perhaps that's why my calling to become a makeup artist and a communicator was so strong.

Mommy and Daddy before I was born

Mommy always found a way to have us dress alike.

I was so blessed to have parents who were amazing in two completely different ways—my mom was the passionate, excitable one who grabbed life by the balls, and my daddy's Zen-like calm was a beautiful counterbalance. I try to honor both of them in the way I live.

I would go to my mom's office with her and see the way she talked to her colleagues—it didn't matter whether it was the president of the hospital, one of her secretaries, or the janitor who emptied the wastebasket. She knew everybody's name and their story—how their mother was recovering from the flu; what college their daughter got in to. When she'd talk to someone, she'd hold their hand and look them right in the eye. When she walked through a room, everyone would stop what they were doing to watch her, not just because she was beautiful (and she was) but because they respected and admired her. I aspired to be like her one day. Years later I found a quote from Maya Angelou that epitomized my mother's philosophy: "I've learned that people will forget what you said, people will forget what you did, but people will never forget how you made them feel." Today it's how I sign off on every email.

And then there is my daddy, who is the most gracious man I have ever met. Whenever we would go to a restaurant and the server would come to our table, Daddy would ask for his or her name. It didn't matter whether we were at a fancy restaurant or the corner deli; he *always* asked their name. He knew that everyone wants to be recognized and appreciated, no matter what their role is.

My mom always made sure that there were lots and lots of parties and picnics for the staff and the patients at the hospital. "Everybody loves a good party!" she'd say. Mommy and Daddy made me come to every one. And participate.

The summer I was seven, Mommy threw a picnic for the center staff and all the patients. Decorations, music, burgers, hot dogs, ice cream stand—the works. I, of course, was at her side while she danced with the patients, sometimes twirling them around in their wheelchairs and singing Whitney Houston songs. She turned to me and said, "Oh, Melissa! Go talk to Helen! You know, she used to be a Rockette! She's beautiful!"

I immediately had this vision of Helen as an elegant, gorgeous older woman, with long, perfect dancer's legs and a great big smile. But when I turned around, there she was, slumped over in her wheelchair, with a little drool hanging out of the side of her mouth. And, honey, those sexy legs hadn't seen a good shave in about twenty years. I didn't know that the hair on a woman's legs could grow that long! And there was some grunting going on.

"Mommy!" I pleaded. "I don't want to. Please don't make me! She's drooling!"

My mom grabbed my arm firmly, her long nails digging into my skin, and pulled me in close.

"Listen to me, *anak,*" she said through gritted teeth. "I don't care what she's doing. Helen is a wonderful, beautiful woman. She is kind and sweet and has had a beautiful life. It is not her fault that this is the hand God has dealt her. We are here to take care of her and bring her joy. That's our job as human beings. Don't ever, *ever* let me hear you judge anyone again by the way they look. You don't know their story. Do you understand?"

My eyes filled with tears, partly because I was embarrassed and partly because her nails were kind of hurting me. She was really mad. I glanced over at my dad; he knew exactly what Mommy was saying and nodded in agreement.

Dynasty era—don't mess with us!

I slowly walked over to Helen and said, "Hi, Ms. Helen. I'm Melissa." She didn't even lift her eyes. "Are you having fun?" No response. I stood there uncomfortably for a minute and tried to think of something else to say.

I mustered up enough courage to reach out and touch her veiny blue hand. "I really like to dance, and my mom said that you used to be a dancer."

Her blue eyes gazed up to the sky. "Yes . . . a Rockette," she whispered. And then she looked at me and smiled!

Helen and I spent the rest of the picnic together. Sure, she would fall asleep sometimes, but when she was alert, she'd tell me bits of stories about her life. I couldn't believe it! I not only made a connection, but I was also really surprised at how happy I felt about it. All of a sudden, it didn't matter what Helen looked like or that she was mentally ill.

That day was when I realized that *everyone* is truly beautiful and that everyone deserves to be treated with love and respect.

I have already begun trying to spread that love to my babies. This year, my dad, my stepmother, Fely, my husband, Phil, and I took our three girls to an assisted-living facility to bring Valentine cards to the residents. I could feel my daughters' apprehension at first, but after some gentle coaxing they went around the room, handing out cards. I saw one of them sitting with a white-haired lady in a wheelchair; the woman was slurring so much that I knew my daughter couldn't understand what she was saying. As I walked over to them, I heard my daughter say to the woman, "Happy Valentine's Day, Miss Fran. You're beautiful." It was one of the proudest moments of my life!

I find myself gravitating toward people who share my parents' philosophy. Take Céline Dion, whose makeup I did for the first time in 2001. She has the same gracious, generous spirit, and she really reminds me of my mom in so many ways, right down to her love of shoes. Even though she's been blessed with huge talent and commercial success, she never forgets the little girl inside her who just wanted to be a singer. I've never seen a celebrity connect so personally with everyone around her, whether she's performing for thousands or hanging out in the green room. She taught me how important it is to respect your children's need for routine and security, and I still thank her for it. When we were working on a video shoot, even if it was going to go all night, we would take our break at her son's bedtime so she could tuck him in. In our house, one of us is always there to tuck the girls in. If it's me, I sing Céline's song "Miracle" to them. If I have to travel, I always try to take a flight that leaves after their bedtime.

I'm blessed to have a career where I get to do the two things I love most: create beauty and connect with people. When you are doing a client's makeup, you are face-to-face, inches apart. Touching someone's skin is an intimate thing. You share energy and feelings. I always feel it is an honor to listen to people's stories while I apply their makeup. We all know that makeup is emotional and powerful. It can change how you feel. On days when you are feeling shitty, it can get you to where you need to be.

> *"Listen to people. Really listen."*

Makeup is my way of communicating, loving, and treating people like superstars. Social media has allowed me to do that on a whole new level. I love sending out inspiring messages, and I can't tell you how many beautiful things I read from my Mallynistas. I marvel at their strength and resilience. We lift one another up.

Over the years of communicating with my Mallynistas, I've also learned to trust their advice on everything from the next color of eye shadow we should create to which jewelry I should wear to a business meeting. And they trust me to give them beautiful makeup that performs the way I say it will. True story: My team and I were struggling to decide which lipstick shade we were going to include in a kit. I posted on Facebook, Instagram, and Twitter a picture of two options. Within five minutes, seven hundred people answered! I used the one that got the most votes—and the kit sold out in eight minutes when it was featured on QVC.

I want to pass on to you my parents' values of respect, love, and connection. Listen to people. Really listen. Call people by their name. And see beauty in everyone. It's always, *always* there.

How to Light Up the Room

You know that beautiful glow you get when you feel healthy or amazing, or when someone makes you feel happy and alive? Well, I'm here to show you how to look luminous even when you feel like crap. And guess what? Seeing is believing. Try this perfect-complexion routine—it's the makeup version of an antidepressant.

1. Start with your usual skin-care routine. Don't forget your SPF!

2. Smooth primer on top. It locks in your moisturizer and creates a smooth, perfect canvas for your foundation and concealer.

3. Concealer is key! It should be one or two shades lighter than your skin tone (but not too pale, or you'll look like you're wearing a mask) to brighten your face. Make sure you use it under your eyes, on the inner and outer corners of the eyes, on either side of the nose, and on either side of the lips for an instant mini face-lift—I swear. If you want to work a little highlighting magic, you can also put concealer between your eyebrows and on your cheekbones, with a touch on your Cupid's bow, chin, and the tip of your nose. Blend well.

4. No matter what kind of foundation you use—liquid, powder, cream, whatever!—the key is to blend, blend, blend, until you can't tell where the foundation ends and your skin begins! Don't forget your jawline and neck. You can use a brush, sponge, or your fingers to apply. Here's how makeup artists get the perfect foundation color for their clients: We match the foundation to your neck or your collarbone. For less coverage, use tinted moisturizer.

5. Set your foundation with a lightweight powder that is not translucent. Why? Because translucent powder is not clear. It's actually white and leaves a ghostly cast. I like a lightly tinted powder, or, for really bulletproof makeup, I use a light dusting of powder foundation.

chapter

3

What Makes You Different Makes You Beautiful

WAS THE ONLY ASIAN GIRL IN MY CLASS AT OUR LADY OF MOUNT Carmel Elementary School. (Okay, technically I'm not Asian. As a Filipino woman, I'm a Pacific Islander by heritage, but my point is that I was the only kid there with tan skin and almond-shaped, up-slanted brown eyes.) It didn't bother me that I didn't look like anybody else, and, like every other kid, I got teased occasionally, but nothing really upsetting or threatening ever happened. Until one day in the third grade.

I took the school bus to and from school every day. Middletown was a small but pretty diverse community, economically and socially, and the bus served both the public and parochial schools in town. By the time it stopped for me, the front rows were full and I would walk to the back. On this day, as I made my way down the aisle, two bigger kids stepped in front of me and blocked my way.

On vacation, around the time I was getting a book bag slammed on my head on the school bus

"Hey, Chink! Where do you think you're going?"

I took a step back. "Could you please let me by?" I ducked my head and squeezed past them.

"Whatever, Fish Lips! We'll get you tomorrow, Flat Face!"

After that, I woke up every school day nervous and upset, knowing what waited for me on the bus. But the more I ignored those kids, the more aggressive the yelling became, and when I still wouldn't react, they hit me over the head with their book bags, tripped me as I walked down the bus aisle, and whacked me on the back as I passed.

I would focus on my seat in the back of the bus, repeating to myself, "Just get there, just get there," over and over. The taunting went on for weeks, and every day I would do everything in my power to drown out that noise and get to my safe seat.

My mom soon realized that something was going on, and one evening she sat me down to talk. I began to cry and spilled the whole story.

Now that I'm the mother of three little girls, I can imagine how infuriated she must have been. I know when I feel my kids are being bullied, my Mama Bear comes out! But she kept her composure and held me tight as I cried.

My fierce parents—always my protectors

"You know, *anak,* sometimes people are afraid of what they don't know. Sometimes things that are different are easy targets. It's our job on earth not to hate or be angry. It's our job to forgive and just remember that we need to be always proud of who we are. I know that there are not a lot of Filipinos in this town, but that is okay. Remember, Melissa, what people need to know is that what makes you different makes you beautiful."

She gave me a hug and I smiled. I took those words into my heart, and I wasn't afraid anymore. I stopped trying to make myself smaller when I walked onto the bus; I stood tall (as tall as I could stand). Instead of looking at the floor as I hurried to my seat, I looked those kids right in the eye. Because I stopped acting like a victim, they stopped treating me like one, and after that the bullying stopped. I had earned their respect.

My mother's incredible words have become a mantra in my life, and I want you to know this too:

What makes you different makes you beautiful. Embrace who you are, what you are, the gifts that God gave you. Those things about yourself that you don't love—you know, your freckles, your laugh lines, your nose—those are the delicious, unique characteristics that make you YOU. And you, my love, are beautiful.

How to Build a Flawless Face

When it comes to feeling strong and confident, knowledge is power. So many people have asked me, "In what order should I apply my makeup? Do I do my eyes first? My foundation?" From concealer to lipstick, here's how I put on a perfect face every time. If you don't use everything here, this order still works.

1. Skin care
2. Primer
3. Concealer
4. Foundation
5. Highlighter
6. Contouring powder
7. Blush
8. Eye shadow
9. Eyeliner
10. Mascara
11. Brow pencil or powder
12. Lip color

chapter

4

Have It Your Way

MY PARENTS INSTILLED IN ME THE DESIRE NOT JUST TO work but to excel at whatever I did. I was fourteen years old when I marched into our local Burger King at the Orange Plaza Mall and talked my way into a job. (Well, I was actually thirteen, but I really wanted that job and told the manager I was fourteen.) I must have been convincing, because I was hired on the spot to be the fry girl.

I've always believed that in order to do the best you can at your job, you have to feel good and look good. When they handed me my uniform, I immediately took it to our tailor, Armando, to give it a couture fit. When I gave him the rust-colored polyester top and pants and told him what I wanted, he said, "Are you kidding me?" I was absolutely not kidding.

I had Armando take in the top so it was fitted and had a little peplum flare, and I asked him to taper the pants so they fit like skinny jeans. Think Audrey Hepburn. I custom-blended a bunch of lipsticks in a pillbox until I had a shade that matched the uniform *exactly*. I called it "BK Brick" and wore it only when I worked. I even glued gold and copper rhinestones to my visor.

It didn't matter that I was in the back working the fryer. I was going to make the best French fries anyone ever had at this Burger King, or at *any* Burger King, for that matter—just enough time in the fryer, piping hot, perfectly crispy, and just the right amount of salt. Not content just to make the best French fries ever, I went on to perfect the milk shake.

But I had bigger dreams. I had my eye on the coveted cashier's spot, and you know I worked my ass off to get there. I wanted to interact with our customers and be their advocate over the microphone, making sure they had the best experience and got everything they wanted, exactly the way that they wanted it.

"Hello, welcome to Burger King. My name is Mally and it's my pleasure to serve you today."

I truly took it to the next level. Every customer was important to me, and I wanted each one to feel at home. "Hello, welcome to Burger King. My name is Mally and it's my pleasure to serve you today. I want you to be happy, so be sure to be honest with me. What would you like to eat?"

Some people found it amusing or endearing; others found me plain annoying, but I didn't care. It was my duty to make sure that I communicated to the kitchen staff their order of a Double Whopper with cheese, no pickles, and extra mayo.

And, you know, to this day I still have the drive to give my Mallynistas the best, whether it's the perfect lip color, an eyeliner that goes on like butter and lasts without smearing for twenty hours, an inspiring tweet, or the most exciting on-air presentation. I'll never forget the young girl I was at the Burger King counter, and, just as she did, I embrace my passion for what I love every single day (and I still bedazzle anything I can).

Find *your* passion. What do you love? I don't care what it is—kittens, cupcakes, cars: Make it your life.

Soft, Natural Makeup for a Young Woman

Everyone asks me when I'm going to let my daughters wear makeup. Contrary to my own experiences at Saks Fifth Avenue and selling burgers with a full face on, they won't be reaching for the foundation and blush until they're in high school. There's a way to wear makeup that's very age-appropriate for a tween and for a young woman. Here's what I'm going to tell the Beans:

The golden rule: Keep a light touch! You want to enhance your fresh, natural beauty, not cover it up!

For a Tween or Young Teen

1. Apply tinted moisturizer all over your face, blending it well into your skin, over your jawline, and toward your neck.

2. If you have blemishes, use a concealer that matches your skin tone, dabbing it on and around any blemishes with a brush.

3. Add one coat of mascara to top and bottom lashes and a sheer lip gloss. Done!

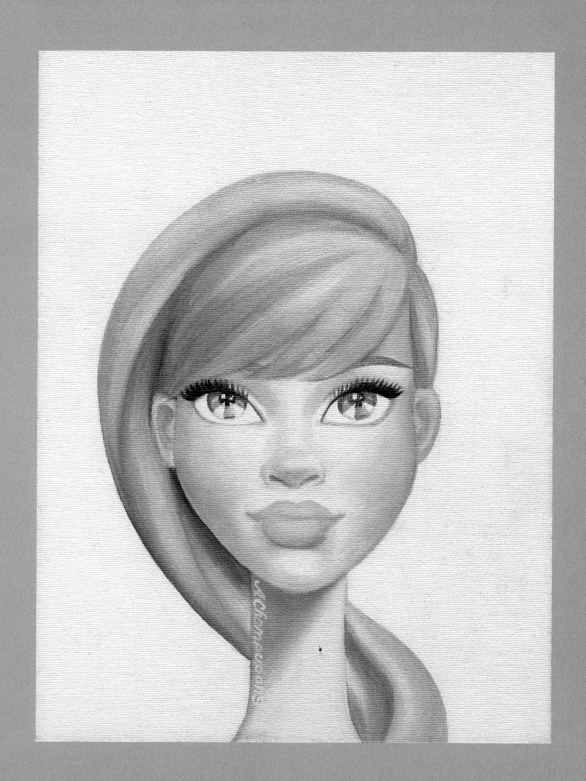

For an Older Teen or Early Twentysomething

1. Cover any dark circles with a concealer that's a shade or two lighter than your skin tone.

2. Conceal any blemishes.

3. Apply a tinted moisturizer or lightweight powder foundation, blending well over your jawline and down toward your neck.

4. Pick a soft peach or pink blush. Use my Cinnamon Bun Method: Apply a little in the middle of the apple of your cheeks, and blend it in larger and larger spirals up and toward your cheekbones.

5. Apply a light matte or shimmery eye shadow from lash line to crease.

6. Curl your lashes and apply two coats of mascara on the top lashes and one coat on the bottom.

7. Finish with a pale, lightweight lip gloss.

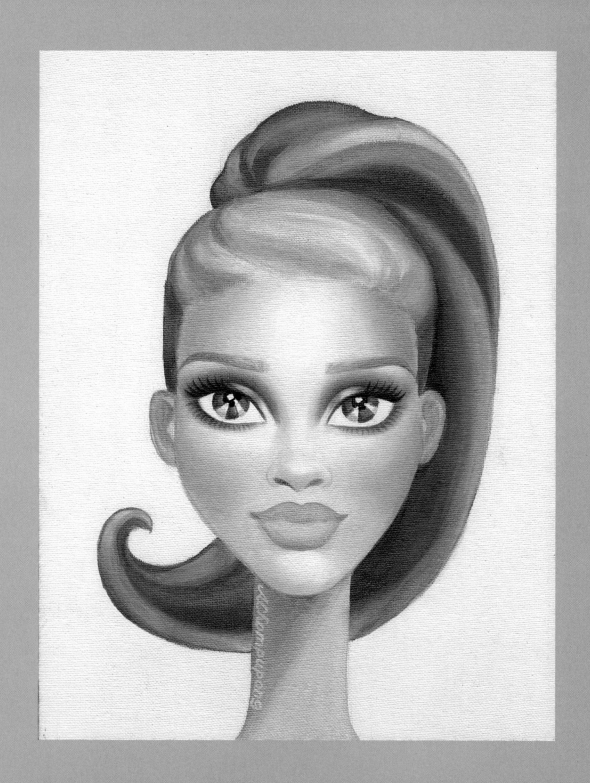

chapter

5

Live Without Regrets

I T WAS JUST A REGULAR DAY. I WAS A SENIOR IN HIGH SCHOOL AND had just gotten home from school. Mommy was in bed and Daddy was already there, sitting next to her. She hadn't been feeling well that day and was having trouble breathing.

"Maybe we should call an ambulance," he said.

"Okay, yes," she whispered between gasps.

I stood by, leaning into the doorway. This was something that had happened before.

I got myself ready for what I knew was about to come. Whenever Mommy had to go to the hospital, I did the same things to make sure she was happy and comfortable. It was my job to pack her nightgowns (she did not feel fashionable in a hospital gown!), her electric blanket (she was always cold, something else that I have inherited from her), and, most important, her makeup. The medical team would be rolling her out our front door on a stretcher, and I would see her perfectly manicured hand with its red nails, sparkling with rings and diamond bracelets, waving at me while she yelled, *"Me-LEE-sa! Pack my makeup!"*

Mommy felt very strongly about having her face on, especially when she was

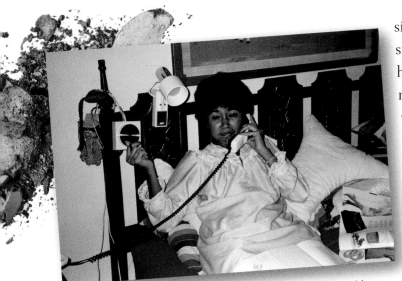

Mommy doing a little catalog shopping. She *always* had her face on.

sick. It didn't matter if she was sick in bed at home or in the hospital. Maybe it was her armor, something she could control when so much else was out of her control. But I do know that she did it for others; even when she was sickest, she wanted to make other people feel comfortable. She knew that if they came to see her and she *looked* sick, they would feel sorry for her and feel bad themselves. She wanted them to feel good. So she put on her pretty face to make them smile and maybe to give them—and her too—hope.

The last time she went to the hospital was the afternoon of March 17, 1989.

As the medical team rolled the stretcher out, I waited for her yell, but she didn't call for me. I smiled and touched her hand as she rolled down the hall. "Want me to pack your makeup, Mommy?" I asked cheerfully.

She slowly opened her eyes and just shook her head. "No, *anak*," she whispered. And I knew this trip to the hospital was going to be different from the ones before.

My heart was throbbing with so many emotions: sadness, worry, fear, anger, confusion. I didn't care what she said. I rushed back to her room to gather her nightgowns, electric blanket, and makeup. I was sure she would want the makeup in the morning when we ate breakfast together and would be happy that I'd brought it.

I raced to the hospital and caught up with Daddy, who had accompanied Mommy in the ambulance, and we walked to her room together, holding hands. When we entered, my mom's eyes locked with Daddy's and she said, "It's done."

He walked over and gave her a hug. What were they talking about? I didn't want to know.

That night, I set myself up to fall asleep in the chair next to her hospital bed, as I had before, and watched her chest heaving up and down as she struggled to breathe. She was such a fighter.

I felt the urge to talk to Daddy, who was sleeping in an empty room down the hall.

"Daddy?"

"What's wrong, honey? Is Mommy okay?"

"Well, she's still breathing hard but she's resting. Daddy, do you think that I should talk to her?"

"I think that that may be a good idea. But do you want to wait 'til morning?"

Something told me no, and I went back into her room. "Mommy? Can you hear me?"

After a few seconds, she lowered her chin as if to say yes.

"I'm going to talk to you, okay, Mommy? Because there are some things that I need you to know. If you hear me, let me know."

She squeezed my hand softly.

"I know that you are tired, Mommy. I know that you have been fighting so hard. I know that for my whole life you have been giving all that you have for me and that you never ever gave up, because you wanted to be there to watch me grow. You are the best mommy that anyone could have ever asked for, and I want you to know that I know that. You have taught me everything that I need to know to be a good adult. You have been the best example of what a woman and mother should be, and I want to be just like you when I grow up. You are my idol and my inspiration, and I promise that if you are tired and you want to go, I'm okay. I promise I will take care of Daddy and myself and make you proud. I will be all right. You can let go and rest."

Two tears escaped from her closed eyes and rolled down her face, and I kissed her cheek.

I sat there for what seemed like hours, staring so hard at her face and hands, trying to burn their image into my brain. Eventually I climbed back into the chair and fell asleep.

All of a sudden I felt a shove on my shoulder that jolted me awake, but when I looked around, nobody was there.

I looked over at my mom; she looked different. Her chest wasn't moving at all. I jumped up and ran to Daddy. When we got back to her room, he put his head on her chest and looked up at me. "Oh, Melissa. She's gone." Our eyes welled up with tears.

At that exact moment, a nurse walked in and checked my mom's vital-signs monitor. "No, not yet. But it's soon. She waited for you." She left the room so we could be alone.

Daddy and I climbed into the bed on either side of her. We hugged her and prayed and just kept saying, "We love you. We love you," over and over. And then she exhaled and let go. It was almost as if I felt her soul leave her body. She floated up to heaven with Daddy and me surrounding her with warmth and love. She was finally at peace.

My mother's death was the most defining moment of my life. It shaped who I was and who I would become. There was not a day that went by that I did not ask why. It changed me. Even as a Catholic girl who attended Catholic school my whole life, it made me question God and whether He really existed. I remember being so mad at him, saying, "I prayed every night to please let her live. Please let her stay with me. I did everything right. I followed every rule. I went to church every Sunday. Why did You let me down?"

Eighteen years later I was sitting with Phil and my daddy in my kitchen. We had just put our twins, Pilar and Sophie, to bed and were taking a much-needed breather. I was telling them how sad I was that Mommy was not there with us to share in the joy of these delicious

My senior prom, without Mommy. It was Daddy and me against the world.

girls, how unbelievable it was to me that she had not been able to meet Phil or to see Mally Beauty come to life. I started to cry, as I had done many, many times since her passing.

"You know, my daughter, sometimes we don't know why the Lord puts situations in our path, but we have to know that He does it for a reason," Daddy said.

What could possibly be the reason to take a mother from her only child? One whom she was so very close to? One for whom she had fought so hard to see grow to be a young woman?

Suddenly it struck us. You see, Mommy and I were *so* close. We had a bond that was *so* strong. We loved as if there was no tomorrow. We joked that I would never leave her side, that I wouldn't even leave to go to college, just so we could stay together.

I think that Mommy knew if she didn't go and let me spread my wings and fly, I wouldn't become the woman I am today. She left so I could go on my journey, with nothing holding me back. She let go so that I could take flight.

When I was willing to accept that, I felt better. I forgave. I understood. And I appreciated. Now, don't get me wrong. It still hurts. I still cry. But I get it. I now know.

What did I learn from these moments in my life? Two of the most valuable lessons that I could ever share with you: First, that God gave me the greatest gift by allowing me to tell Mommy how I felt about her and to say goodbye. There was nothing left unsaid between us. I have no regrets. I can live the rest of my life until I see her again knowing that she knew how grateful I was to have her as my mother and how much I loved her. Please, please, *please:* Do not let the people you love leave this earth without telling them how you feel about them. Make sure your loved ones know how you feel. Every day.

And, second, sometimes shitty things happen. Sometimes you are in so much pain, you can't even find words to describe it. Your heart hurts so much that you feel like it will never go away. But it does. Everything happens for a reason, even though when you are in it you can't see why and all you can feel is the pain. But, please, just know this. It may take weeks, months, even years. But one day, as I did, you will understand, you will forgive. And you will heal.

chapter

If It Doesn't Work, Let It Go

W HEN I WAS IN COLLEGE, I WAS *OBSESSSSSSSED* WITH ALL things fierce.

My friends and I had a weekend club ritual that always started at the Roxy on 18th Street. We only went to the gay clubs.

Club days

I had no interest in drugs or drinking. The atmosphere was what gave me my high. I loved the glamour, the freedom. I loved watching all of the amazing people. And the drag queens! They took hair, makeup, and super-feminine style to the next level.

This Saturday night at the club was extra-fabulous.

I was super-excited because I had bought a new outfit for this night. I was going for a little sixties' glam—I wore a psychedelic, Pucci-inspired print hot-pants-and-halter-top suit, white patent knee-high platform boots, and a candy-apple-red wig styled in a flip with a white headband. My makeup was classic sixties—powder-blue shadow popped with a little iridescent glitter on the lid, black liquid liner, round brows, and white-pink frosty lips.

One couple totally caught my eye. They were ah-*maaa*-zing. One of them was tall and slim, white, with the longest legs I had ever seen. The other was shorter, exotic, and tan—could she be Filipina? They were dressed as Super Outer Space Pink-and-Purple Pleather Bond Girls.

Zaldy and Mathu. My Fairy Drag Godmothers!

I marched over to them in my gigantic platform shoes as fast as my feet could carry me, reached out, and tapped on the thigh of the tall white one.

"Excuse me . . . *excuse me*!"

He looked down his nose at me, probably appalled, amazed, and flattered at this ballsy little girl who had the nerve to disturb his club time. "Pardon me?"

I said, "You are *so* gorgeous! I love everything about you— your hair, your clothes, your styling, your makeup! I want you to adopt me so I can learn how to do what you do!" I was kidding (sort of), but they did take me under their very colorful wings that night.

Those amazing creatures were Mathu and Zaldy. They were a gay couple and major players in the art and nightlife scene in New York City. They did it all: hair, makeup, styling, and photography, and they were the geniuses collaborating with the legendary RuPaul on her look. (And I was right—Zaldy is from the Philippines!) Their creativity was a never-ending source of inspiration for me.

One day I was hanging out at their apartment at the Hotel Chelsea when Mathu came home from a job and started telling Zaldy and me about his day, in his gorgois Australian accent.

"I was doing a job with Claudia Schiffer today. You know, she has the most incredible hair. It's like super blond in the front, a warmer blond in the middle, and dark blond in the back."

I saw the glimmer in his eye as he stared me down, eyeing my long black hair. Zaldy giggled. He knew what Mathu was thinking.

I just started shaking my head. "No, no, no, *nooooo* . . . no way . . ." I was *not* going to be an art project.

Eight hours later, I stepped out of their shower, with platinum-blond hair.

Toga! Toga! Toga!

I can hear the sizzle . . . .

That's me in the middle. Let it go!

Needless to say, that art project became my signature look. I *loved* being different and I wanted to never let it go.

But I have to tell you, when you have platinum-blond hair and your natural hair color is black, those roots are *major*! Sometimes I could see black roots the day after I got my hair done! Mathu wasn't always available to touch them up, so I would ask some of my other friends, hair-care professionals or not, to do it for me. Hell, what did we need? Some 100-volume peroxide and some tinfoil? Done! It got to the point where the bleach would burn my scalp and I'd have scabs after every session, but, as RuPaul said when he was being sewn into a corset, beauty is pain, dahling!

But all good things come to an end. One day, I enlisted one of my friends to do my roots at my apartment.

"I don't know, Mally. Your hair looks a little bit fried."

"Whatever. Just do it!"

We put the bleach in and it started to burn my scalp, as usual. I just fanned my head with magazines and sang really loudly to distract myself.

When it was time to rinse the bleach out, I stuck my head under the faucet of the kitchen sink and—what the *hell*?

My hair started breaking off in my hands like big chunks of wet vermicelli. Chunks and chunks, more and more. My friend started screaming.

"I told you! I told you!! I said your hair couldn't take it!!"

I had to laugh so I wouldn't cry! When it was all said and done, I had a VERY interesting bleach "chemical cut." It was like a reverse Mohawk. The entire center of my head was about an inch long, but the sides were still long to my shoulders. Then there was my hairline. That was kind of short and bristly too. All around my head.

And that, my friends, was the end of my days as a platinum blonde.

YOU KNOW, I'VE ALWAYS been *that* girl—the one who would wear the gravity-defying platform shoes, the colorful tights or fishnets, black-rimmed Buddy Holly glasses (with plain glass lenses so I could wear my contacts, of course), just because I liked the look. I would dye my hair colors not found in nature, shave off my eyebrows so I could draw them back wherever I liked, perm my lashes—whatever!

It was the nineties, and it was the cool thing to have long acrylic tips on your nails. My girlfriend Candy and I decided that we were going to go authentic; we would take the train uptown to Harlem and get it done by the pros. We were going to be *SER*-VING!

We found a salon where the homegirls went. We could not *believe* how many amazing airbrush options they had: flowers, beach scenes, faces, rainbows, stars, clouds—how could we choose? A fierce black girl, Shaneece, who had the most incredible nails (white, painted with beach scenes complete with palm trees), took care of me, popping her gum and telling me as she went to work that she was the best in town.

I had settled on looooong fake nails (they had to be an inch and a half long) with super-square edges,

My first boss, Kalinka

creamy polish, and big, fabulous red, orange, and yellow flames airbrushed on each nail. The pièce de résistance was "Mally" airbrushed in Old English calligraphy on each thumbnail. I mean, come *on*! I was in love!

We walked out of the salon in all our giddy glory and hailed a cab. When it stopped, neither one of us could open the car door! I couldn't work my flip phone or pick up a grape either, and wiping my butt became an act that would make a contortionist proud. Sorry, but it's true! I didn't care, though. I loved my nails and how cool I felt with them on. Who needs grapes or phone calls anyway?

"WHAT is going on with those nails?"

A couple of days later, I got a call to assist the legendary Bobbi Brown at a fashion show in the tents at Bryant Park during Fashion Week in New York City. Brown was a makeup artist who had started her own eponymous product line; she was a major inspiration to me. I was super-excited and so honored that I would be working as a member of her team. Since I was freelance and didn't have a kit of her makeup, I'd be sharing with another artist.

When I arrived backstage, I was introduced to Bobbi. And, you know, for all her success and accomplishments and power in the industry, she was warm and welcoming (and really tiny and cute!). And she said that I could share *her* kit. I'd be working next to Bobbi Brown HERSELF!

Bobbi grabbed a model and demonstrated the look we'd be creating for the show. It was the classic Bobbi face: perfect skin, thick black liner on the upper lash line only, and brown lipstick. At the fashion shows, the head makeup artist demos on a single girl the look that all the models will wear. The team watches, and then they're set free to re-create that vision on their own in the midst of the backstage chaos. Sometimes they get it right the first time, and sometimes an artist has to redo the model three or four times until the head artist is satisfied.

When Bobbi was done, I cozied right up to her and prepared to get down and dirty. I was going to do *everything* in my power to impress her! I reached down to the palette to get some concealer on my ring finger. Oh, no. This was going to be a challenge.

Bobbi looked at me, obviously kind of horrified, yet maybe also a little bit amused. "*What* is going on with those nails?"

"They're fake! Aren't they cool?" I said, holding them up for her to admire.

"Absolutely, definitely not," her face said. "How are you going to do makeup with them?" she asked instead.

I had to admit to myself, I wasn't completely sure. But with a lot of maneuvering and lots of brushes, I made it through the show.

As soon as I got home that night, I bid a fond farewell to my fabulous nails and cut them off. They were fun, and fierce, and totally me, but I didn't need anything in my life that made things harder, not easier.

Sometimes we have to learn the hard way to let something go. I learned that lesson (twice!) at the cost of my hair (and a little bit of my dignity) and a set of very expensive fake nails. It doesn't have to happen to you. Knowing who you are means knowing what looks good on you and being willing to change when it doesn't work for you anymore. Are you still wearing a hard-edged lip liner? Let it go. Still using dark-brown streaks down your cheeks to "contour"? Let it go. And it's not just about the makeup. The "friends" who don't support you? Let them go too.

My Two Most Timeless Techniques

What makeup looks *never* go out of style? Natural eyeliner and flattering, healthy-looking blush. They make every woman look polished and fresh. Master them, and you'll be set for life.

Natural Eyeliner

1. The biggest mistakes I see women making when it comes to eyeliner are using a very heavy, hard-edged line and using the same color on the top and bottom lashes. The secret is to use two different-colored eyeliners, with the darker color on the top and the lighter on the bottom (examples: black on top, brown on the bottom; dark brown or plum on top, bronze on the bottom; dark gray or navy on top, light taupe on the bottom).

2. Make sure your pencils are sharp. On the upper lid, sketch a skinny line going deep into the lashes, starting from the outer corner to the inner corner. This defines the lashes and makes them look thicker without making the eye look droopy.

3. Take an eyeliner brush, cotton swab, or your finger, and gently feather the line to soften it.

4. Line the lower lash line with the lighter-color eyeliner, burying the line as deep into the lower lashes as possible. Gently smudge or feather the line to soften it.

Blush

1. You can never go wrong with a soft matte or shimmer pink or peach blush (if you have fair skin, look for blush with a silvery shimmer; if you have darker skin, a warmer golden shimmer is flattering). If you're using a powder blush, a natural bristle brush will give you the most natural application. For a cream blush, use a brush with synthetic bristles; it "grabs" the product, for a more even application with fewer streaks. If you use your fingers, just be sure to blend *really* well.

2. Look in the mirror and smile so you can see the "apples" of your cheeks.

3. Tap the brush into your blush and tap off the excess product (don't blow it off!).

4. Use my Cinnamon Bun Method: Start with a little in the middle, and with a circular motion blend blend blend out and up toward the cheekbones, making the circles bigger as you go.

chapter

7

Bee Calm

F YOU SEE ME ONLY ON QVC, YOU PROBABLY THINK I'M LIKE THE Energizer Bunny on Red Bull, constantly on the go. And, honestly, sometimes it feels that way. But life is a marathon, not a sprint, and we all need to find a place of calm to think and recharge, even if it isn't easy to find that space in our crazy lives.

There are so many things that I have learned from my sweet daddy. I can be in the middle of trying to wrestle with a problem for days and just can't figure it out. I call Daddy, give him the rundown, and he always seems to know the right answer. I am so grateful to have been raised by a man of such intellectual and spiritual intelligence. Phil affectionately and respectfully calls my dad "Confucius."

Daddy and his crazy beans

Daddy <3 Always my idol.

In the early nineties, I was living on my own in a tiny apartment in Greenwich Village and had brought some friends back home to Middletown. It was always so nice to get out of the city, get a home-cooked meal, and do some laundry. My stepmom, Fely, and my dad were always welcoming and happy to see us.

It was a hot summer day and we were all chilling by the pool—my friends Alisa, Candace, Cliff, and Michael. A bumblebee came buzzing over and got in our personal space. All of us, being a *tad* dramatic (surprise!), started *freaking out*. I mean screaming and yelling and running around, arms flailing.

My dad, who was sitting there calmly, said peacefully, "Kids, kids. Stop. Just relax. You are doing this all wrong."

When we finally stopped screaming and running around, he looked at us with compassion.

"My kids. Can I give you some advice? A bee is like life."

Huh?

"Like life. When a bee comes around—when there is chaos or something scary comes your way—instead of screaming or running, just sit and be still. What is meant to be will be." (I

About two minutes before that bee flew in and scared the crap out of us

don't even think he knew how punny that was!) "The universe and God will take care of you in your peaceful state. You just have to believe." (Again with the puns!)

And then, almost as if on cue, that bee flew over to my dad and started buzzing around his head! He looked right at it and said calmly, "Hello, bee." And don't you know that that bee just about-faced and flew away?

My friends and I sat there with our mouths hanging open.

"See?" he said, and smiled.

To this day, whenever things get crazy, when I have two shoots and a live TV show scheduled, the Beans have Girl Scouts, and I have three deadlines for magazine stories, or when I can't get that new eye shadow color just right, I say, "Hello, bee." And it makes me feel better.

Trust, believe, and don't try to control what you can't control. Don't panic! It's not what happens to you that is important. It's how you react.

"What is meant to be will be."

A QUICK CONFESSION

Okay, I'm going to admit it: I am a worrier. Ugh. It pains me to even type it. Even with my dad's calming influence, even when I'm saying "Hello, bee," my mind can still race with thoughts of what might go wrong.

As a kid, I worried about my mom, whether my hair looked good, how I was doing in school (yes, in that order). As I got older, my worries got bigger: my career, growing my business, my kids.

I'm an equal-opportunity worrier. I can worry about anything. What I said or didn't say; how I'm going to handle that unpleasant conversation. Am I a good mama? Are the Beans happy? Did Phil drink enough water? (Did I?) How's that new eyeliner coming? Is it really good enough for my Mallynistas? How can I make it better? Did I leave the stove on? My daddy didn't email back. Is he okay? This is a typical conversation that happens in my head as I lie in bed with the lights out, trying to get to sleep, or in the car. I used to think that worrying like this was just thinking. This is not thinking.

Worrying is the enemy. It sucks the life out of us. I once read, "Worrying does not take away tomorrow's troubles, it takes away today's peace." A-*men*.

And you know what? Worrying is not doing any favors for our faces. One day, I was sitting in my office "enjoying" one of my "bunching sprees." (That's my daddy's psychiatrist term for when you worry about everything at once and all your problems seem impossible to overcome.) I looked up and caught a glimpse of myself in the mirror, and I looked like a prune! My brows were furrowed; my lips were pursed. The "number 11" wrinkles between my eyebrows were two deep trenches. I looked mad. And stressed. Whoa! Years of that could cause some serious damage! (On the other hand, there are some beautiful lines, like laugh lines, that show up on our faces after years of happiness. They're your badges of honor.) I immediately straightened up and stretched out my face.

I used to get so mad at Phil! Well, not mad, more like envious. He can fall asleep anytime, no matter what he's got going on. When I asked how he does it, he said, "Why worry? It's going to be there tomorrow, and there's nothing I can do about it now. So let's just get some rest so we are strong enough tomorrow to fight!" Very smart, but—let's admit it—easier said than done.

There's one thing that has helped me deal with my worry problem: faith.

One of my favorite sayings is: "Let your faith be bigger than your fear." I try to remember that there isn't enough space in our hearts and souls for both faith and worry, and when I let faith in, I put my trust in God (or the universe or a Higher Power, whichever you believe in) that what happens will be the best for me. If you're a worrier like me, take some time today and try to focus on your faith. It's stronger and more powerful than we are. Let it go, breathe, and believe.

Look, I know it's not easy. Even as I write this, my brain is saying, *Hmmm, I hope that I'm getting this right. I hope that I'm giving them good information. I hope that I'm inspiring them. Did I leave the stove on?* Oh, jeez! But if you promise to keep trying, so will I!

I WAS SO FORTUNATE that my parents saw who I was and told me that the right thing to do was to follow my own path, even though sometimes my passion for makeup felt frivolous in comparison to what they did. My "aha" moment didn't come until years later.

I was home visiting with Daddy and Fely, and we were watching a television show about the strides doctors were making in curing cancer.

I turned to my dad. "Great," I said. "Look at all of the amazing things that you doctors do, and look at me! All I do is put mascara on people for a living!"

The Wise Ones: Daddy and my stepmother, Fely

My dad stared at me with an expression on his face that I had never seen before, a mix of disbelief and anger.

"Melissa! I can't believe that I am hearing what you are saying. Don't you *ever* discount what you do in your life! By putting makeup on people, you are helping them feel good. You are giving them confidence and ammunition to go further in life. You can help them heal their souls. You put makeup on them, yes, but you also teach them how to look and feel good so that they may go out and lead better lives and affect other people! Don't ever let me hear you say that again!"

Wow.

I took my dad's message to heart. No matter what God puts into your heart, don't ignore it. Don't question it. He put it in there for a reason. Because that's what your contribution to this world is. No matter who you are or where you are in life, you have talents and a voice. Use them. You have the opportunity to affect other people's lives in a positive way; do it.

And that's important, because *you* are important.

From that day forward, I never *ever* belittled or underestimated the importance of what I do for a living. I know that some people out there think that what I do is silly, that makeup is just for people who are insecure or who don't love themselves, people who want to hide. Pardon my French, but that is bullshit! To me, makeup is about feeling good, looking good, caring about yourself, and showing the world that you want to put your best face forward.

> **"By putting makeup on people, you are helping them feel good. You are giving them confidence and ammunition to go further in life."**

Makeup empowers a woman to present herself in exactly the way she chooses. She is the one deciding, and I can give her the tools and the power to do that. When a woman tells me she put on my lip gloss and it made her feel beautiful, I know that change is more than skin deep.

How to Look Calm (When You're Super Stressed)

When life gets nutty, our faces might tell stories we don't really want them to tell. Droopy eyes and dark circles are the telltale signs that you're feeling overextended and a little cray cray. Here are my two secret weapons—mascara and concealer—for looking calm, confident, and wide awake!

Master Mascara

There are so many different kinds of mascara: volumizing, lengthening, defining, separating, thickening, waterproof, not waterproof—how do you choose? I don't think you can ever go wrong with a volumizing formula that gives you thick, long, full, beautiful lashes. No matter how frugal you are, replace your mascara after three months—otherwise, it becomes a breeding ground for bacteria.

1. Black mascara is always my first choice. If you have super, super, super fair hair and skin, black-brown will give you a softer, more natural look.

2. Always curl your lashes! It will make you look a zillion times more awake! I use the three-pump method: Start at the base of your lashes, pull out, do the middle, pull out, and squeeze the curler on the tip of the lash. I do this every single day!

3. Pull out your mascara wand. Be sure not to pump the mascara wand into the tube. It gets air into the tube, which also breeds bacteria. Yuck!

4. Hold the wand at the base of your top lashes. Wiggle the mascara wand a little and gently pull it through. Pull the lashes—all of them—in toward the bridge of your nose. This is a top-secret technique: It fans the lashes open, giving your eyes a wide-eyed, starburst effect. If you want a more-sultry look, pull the lashes out toward your temples.

5. I *always* put mascara on the bottom lashes. Hold the wand horizontally and comb down through your lashes or sculpt each lash by holding the wand vertically.

6. Do one or two coats of mascara on the top and one coat on the bottom, and—mega-lashes!

Conceal Dark Circles

Concealer is your BEST FRIEND! Whatever form you prefer (pencil, stick, cream, liquid in a tube), choose one that's a shade or two lighter than your skin tone.

1. Dip a brush or your ring finger (it has the lightest touch) into concealer and warm it up on the back of your hand. This will make it nice and smooth.

2. Gently spread the concealer underneath your eyes and on the inner and outer corners.

3. Press, press, press it into the skin until you can't tell your skin from the concealer. Optional: Set it with a lightweight setting powder specifically made for under the eyes.

chapter

8

Do
the Hustle

SOMETIMES THINK THAT I WAS BORN WITH A MAKEUP BRUSH IN MY hand. I remember being happiest sitting with my mother at her vanity table, watching her put on her face. I was the girl who did everyone's makeup for prom. I was the girl cornering you in the school bathroom to have a go at popping your zits and getting scolded by the nuns at my Catholic school for wearing blue eyeliner in seventh grade. When we were finally allowed to wear makeup in high school, I put on foundation, powder, eye shadow, eyeliner, mascara, lipstick, and lip gloss. Every day.

But while makeup was my love and my passion, putting it on other people didn't seem like a "real" job. My parents were doctors, and I wanted to be like them, so I studied pre-med in college. The problem was that I kind of sucked at it. Did I *reallllly* have to slice up animals to graduate? Yikes!

When it was clear I wasn't, uh, meant to be a doctor, I decided that fashion design was the way to go. Of course, my dad—bless him—was perfectly under-standing. "Follow your heart," he said. "That's what Mommy would have wanted for you too."

Well, have you ever tried to design, drape, and sew a blazer from a pattern you cut yourself? That's harder than cutting up a frog!

After graduating with a degree in fashion design, I got a job working as a design assistant for a designer named Kalinka in New York City. Kalinka was sweetly outrageous, tall and slender, with flaming red hair and pale skin. She was also an amazing talent, and I learned so much from her. Although her clothes were very wearable—Asian-inspired velvet jackets and pants—all her runway shows had a fantasy element, with dramatic theatrical makeup and elaborate hair. She was one of the few designers to have drag queens walk the runway in her shows.

But no matter how busy I was at work, I could never stop thinking that what I *really* wanted to do was makeup. I even took a part-time job at the Shiseido counter at the original Barneys store, on West 17th Street.

Kalinka

My first job out of college. I couldn't have asked for a better experience.

A few months after graduation, my friend Mathu finally said, "You should do it."

Mathu was a makeup artist, but I still said to him, without thinking, "Being a makeup artist is not a real job. That's just *fun*."

He looked at me with his left eyebrow raised as high as his hairline and calmly said, "I just made ten thousand dollars a day doing the Louis Vuitton campaign."

Oh, *snap*! I guess that *is* a "real" job!

By now I was working full time for Tracy Reese, a successful young

our first Polaroid - 3/17/95 xoE

Starting my career as a freelance makeup artist

designer. I knew that if I was going to make my dream my career, I had to hustle. I left Tracy's company (she and I have become good friends, and she's graciously asked me to do her Fashion Week shows for many years) and took every single job that I was offered, paid and not paid. I did every all-night music-video shoot. I did every tiny little picture in *any* magazine. I did how-to exercise pictures. I did kids. I did *dogs*. I put makeup on anything that was not nailed to the floor. And I loved every single second of it.

Word started to spread quickly that I worked hard, showed up on time, never complained about long hours or less-than-perfect working conditions, and was grateful for the work and the experience. I learned quickly that a great attitude will get you far. And get you hired again.

MALLY H. RONCAL
MAKE-UP ARTIST

My business card

Shoots, shoots, and more shoots

The opportunities got better, and so did I; on every job I learned something new about myself and my art and craft. I was getting super-busy. This was still the beginning of my journey, but I learned so many important lessons that I want to pass on to you.

Any work is a real job; be humble and never say no to an opportunity—nothing is beneath you if you're working toward a goal, and we all have to pay our dues. Put simply, always keep your eyes on the prize, and there's no way you won't win.

How to Look Fierce in 2 (or 5, or 10) Minutes Flat

Okay, my loves, you know that if you want to accomplish a dream, ya gotta be a hustla, and ya gotta be ready to hop on the drop of a dime. One of my biggest secrets is to have a makeup strategy ready, no matter how little time you have to get ready. Here are my suggestions for three quick looks—feel free to customize them to suit your own preferences. The more you practice them, the faster and easier they'll get.

The 2-Minute Face

1. Cleanse and moisturize your skin.

2. Apply concealer (see page 62).

3. Tap your brush into a powder foundation and tap off the excess. Buff the foundation into your skin all over your face.

4. Apply one coat of mascara to top and bottom lashes.

The 5-Minute Face

In addition to the 2-Minute Face:

1. Put on another coat of mascara.

2. Quickly fill in your eyebrows. They don't have to be perfect (see page 190).

3. Use the natural-eyeliner technique to line your upper lashes.

4. Apply cream or powder blush (see page 50).

The 10-Minute Face

In addition to the 5-Minute Face:

1. Dab eye shadow base on the eyelid. Using an eye shadow stick or powder eye shadow in shimmering brown, taupe, or dusky plum (no electric blue or teal, please), apply shadow all over the eyelid, from the lash line to the crease, and blend with a brush, using a windshield-wiper motion. Smudge the shadow under the lash line and blend.

2. Dust highlighter powder on your cheekbones—to lift and brighten the eye area—and on the tip of your nose.

My Classic Hollywood Face

There's one look that's in every makeup artist's arsenal of "things you must know how to do," and I call it the classic Hollywood face—a defined brow, liquid cat-eye liner, and a matte red lip. It's a foolproof look for a special night out, or you can tone it down a bit by using a sheer red gloss instead of red lipstick.

1. Apply foundation. You want a satin finish—not too dewy and not matte.

2. Add a little highlighter on the cheekbones. Make a "fish face" and sweep shaping powder in the hollows under your cheekbones (like we did our blusher in the eighties). Use a tiny bit of buff-toned or tawny blush on the apples of your cheeks; it's the contour that's the focus here.

3. Smooth eye shadow base from lash to brow.

4. Apply a shimmery champagne shadow from lash to brow.

5. Add a soft matte taupe shadow in the crease, using a windshield-wiper motion, to contour the lid.

6. Smudge the same taupe shadow under your bottom lashes with a smudger brush.

7. Here's a cat eye made easy: Using a sharp black pencil, line your upper eyelashes from the inner corner out, making the line flip up just before you reach the end of the outer corner of the eye. This will keep your eyes from looking droopy.

8. Now take black liquid liner and drag it gently over the pencil line. Lower your lid and gently fan it so the liner dries and doesn't transfer to your upper lid.

9. If you want to, wear false eyelashes (see page 112 for instructions),

"marry" them to your own lashes with a coat of mascara. Otherwise, add two or three coats of mascara to your upper lashes and one coat to your bottom lashes.

10. Fill in your eyebrows (see page 190). This is the time to go a smidge darker or larger than your natural brow, especially if you're wearing this as an evening look.

11. To create the perfect red lip, first choose your red shade. My rule of thumb: If you mostly wear silver jewelry, select a cooler, blue-based or even a plummy red. If you wear a lot of gold jewelry, look for a warmer, tomatoey red. If you wear both gold and silver jewelry, try a neutral red. I like to apply red lipstick right from the bullet, blot it, then use a matching red lip liner to sharpen and define the outline of the mouth.

OPEN MOUTH, INSERT LOUBOUTIN

I didn't assist many makeup artists early in my career, but when I did, I really enjoyed the experience. I always learned something—a new brand, a new way to use color, a new technique. But one lesson I learned had nothing to do with makeup.

I was helping out on a music video. When you're on set, there's always a lot of downtime. You sit around, drink a lot of coffee, graze at the craft-services table, talk a lot, read magazines. During one of many breaks, I was flipping through a magazine.

Like so many young and inexperienced people, I had a *lot* of opinions, and I had no problem voicing them (no matter how silly or uninformed they might have been). Looking at a fashion story, I decided that I was going to give my critique on how the makeup artist had done the models. "Gosh, what is up with these eyebrows? What's going on with this lipstick? And this blush! Jeez, you'd think the makeup artist put it on with a snow shovel!"

As I talked, the room became eerily silent, and I got a sick feeling in my stomach. I slowly and reluctantly looked up and saw exactly what I was afraid I would see. The makeup artist I was assisting was glaring at me, as was the hairstylist, *his* assistant, *and* the clothing stylist. I looked back down at the credits and, sure enough, there was his name. Open mouth, insert giant platform-clad foot. I felt like crying, puking, and running away at the same time. Seriously, I wanted to D-I-E.

I finished up the rest of the day and barely said a word, except for a whole lot of "I'm so sorry" and "I don't know what I was thinking" and "I didn't mean to insult you." Do I need to tell you that I never heard from this man again?

It's easy to think that everyone in the room wants to hear your words of wisdom, but, to be honest, most of the time, unless people are asking you directly, they probably do not. I'm pretty sure that my unprofessional behavior did not really hurt anyone but me, and I'm unbelievably lucky it didn't seem to affect the path of my career.

If this experience taught me anything, it is this: Very simply, think before you speak. *Make sure you taste those words before you spit them out.* Think about the way *you'd* feel if someone said something to or about you. Are your words hurtful or uplifting? Are they positive or venomous? Are they respectful or rude? So be careful. Something you say could make or break someone's day.

Work it!

chapter

Believe in Happily Ever After

WAS TWENTY-FOUR YEARS OLD, AND I WAS JUST BEGINNING TO really get a groove on in my freelance makeup career.

It was kind of fun—some days I'd be on a job from 6:00 A.M. to 9:00 P.M., and others I'd have nothing to do (like on a Tuesday!). It was a big difference from the Monday-through-Friday gig as a design assistant that I had right out of college.

My fairy tale came true on Monday, October 9, 1995.

That morning I was hanging out having coffee with one of my best friends, Michael. He, his partner, Cliff, and I were inseparable. Michael and I were planning on going to the movies to see *Showgirls* that afternoon (ahhh, the freelance life!), when my phone rang. It was my friend who was a booker (the person who assigns models to shoots) at a modeling agency. He was in a panic.

"Mally! It's me! One of my models is at a job and the makeup didn't show up! The photog is freaking out. Can you go?"

"Well, I may have a gig. . . . I'm just waiting to hear," I said as I winked at Michael.

"Ugh. Okay, well, can you at least call the photographer? His name is Phil

Bickett. Maybe you can go for a minute or suggest someone? Here's his number, and, by the way, he's *really* cute."

When I hung up, I looked at Michael and said, "We're definitely gonna catch this movie, but let me call anyway."

I dialed the number, and someone picked up on the first ring.

I heard this delicious yet panicked Southern drawl. "I'm about to jump out the window."

"Oh, man, well, okay, hi. I'm Mally. I hear you have an issue."

"Yes, I'm sitting here all ready to go, and my makeup artist didn't show up. Can you come over?"

"Don't jump!" I called up. "I'm here."

He sure did *sound* cute. But I really had my heart set on seeing that movie.

"Actually, I can't. Maybe I'll call you later and see if you still need a hand. If you do, then I'll stop by. Sorry."

"All right, maybe we can work together some other time. Thanks for calling anyway."

I hung up and turned to Michael. "Poor guy. He sounds like he's *not* having a good day."

"You know, Mal, maybe you should go. He needs help, and you could use the money. We can see the movie tomorrow."

I sighed and picked up the phone. "Hi, Phil? This is Mally. I'll be right over. Where are you?"

Clip clop clip clop went my white Candie's mules on the sidewalk as I walked from my railroad apartment on Bleecker Street in Greenwich Village to West 11th Street. I was carrying my MAC makeup box and wearing black nylon boot-cut pants and a gray tank top; my platinum-blond hair was curled and pinned to one side. I had thrown on a quick face, but for me that meant drama for daytime. I went for a plum smoky eye and wine lipstick. You know, natural.

When I got to the apartment building, I looked up and saw a man hanging out of a big window. I knew it had to be Phil.

"Don't jump!" I called up. "I'm here."

He smiled big and said, "I'm on the fifth floor." Thankfully, it was an elevator building!

The door to apartment 5G was ajar. I pushed it open with my Candie's-clad foot and said, "So, do you love me?" (Sarcastically, *obviously*.)

He said, "Yes, I love you."

My friend did not lie. Phil Bickett was handsome: tall, slim, not too muscular but definitely built. He had short dark hair with a little bit of gray in it. His face was tan and a teeny bit weathered, kind of like a really hot cowboy. He was a model, but he was following his dream to become a photographer. And that accent—come *on*!

Phil introduced me to the crew and we got to work. Turned out the job was for a lingerie company, and we were shooting this ridiculously amazing eighteen-year-old model in a thong all day. Let's be honest—even if I did think he was cute (and I did!), who can compete with *that*?

We were all over the West Village, shooting on rooftops and side streets. Mr. Phil and I got along really well, cracking each other up constantly. He would set the shot, start shooting, look over at me, and we'd start talking.

At the end of the day, everyone was getting their things together and saying goodbye. I was glad that I had come; I could always go to the movies another day.

Phil walked over to me. "Okay, so let's go to dinner."

No. Way. "Look, that was a great day and all, but I'm not going to go to dinner with you. I just met you."

"You might as well go to dinner with me, because you are going to marry me someday."

Wait. What? I mean, I could feel that we had been getting along, we'd laughed a lot, and

Phil and I, just after we met.

there had definitely been a bit of an attraction—but marry? Wasn't he rushing things just a little?

Funny thing was, I knew he was right. I had this tickle deep in my tummy that I'd never felt before, and I could see us growing old together. And while I'd had some dates (but nothing serious), no one had ever looked at me the way Phil was looking at me now.

That fateful day was just over eighteen years ago. And you know what? It truly *was* love at first sight. From that moment on, unless Phil Bickett and I have been separated for work, we have never slept apart.

I believe that if you live with an open heart and trust that you are meant for the best in the world, you will get it. Don't ever settle. I'm not talking about knight-in-shining-armor, princess-saving shit. I mean that great things can happen if you just believe. I wasn't looking for the man of my dreams that day. I was simply helping out someone who needed it. And you know what else? I got a lot more than a fairy tale. Phil Bickett is my love, my rock, my best friend, my soldier, and my partner in life, parenting, and business. He is my inspiration, my court jester, my psychiatrist. His honesty and integrity make me want to be a better person every day. He is everything that I could have asked for and more. So trust. Have faith. Believe in happily ever after. Just allow your heart to be free, be a good person, live with an honest soul, and God will put all the right opportunities and people right in front of you.

Our first apartment

On our wedding day

Work, Love, Play

Man-Friendly Makeup

Let's be honest. Guys always say they love us without any makeup, but what they really mean is that they like it when we don't *look* as if we're wearing any makeup—when our faces are soft, satiny, and sun-kissed. Here's how to get that bare-but-beautiful look:

1. Spot-conceal dark circles and any blemishes.

2. Brush a light dusting of powder foundation over your face to warm up the skin.

3. Apply gold or bronze eye shadow all over your lid, from lash line to crease, and blend out.

4. Brush a little of the same eye shadow underneath your bottom lashes and blend.

5. Add one coat of mascara on top and bottom.

6. Dab a light shimmery shadow or highlighter on the inner corners of your eyes.

7. Swirl a soft-pink blush on the apples of your cheeks.

8. Finish with a soft-pink tinted lip balm.

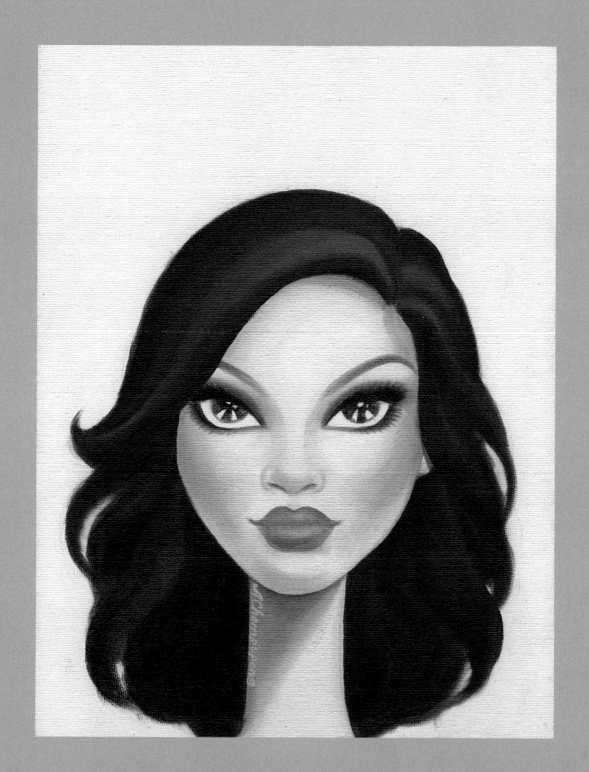

Big-Day Makeup

Is there anything more romantic than a wedding? My approach for this most special day is an innocent, soft, and dewy look. I use makeup with sheer textures and give cheeks and lips a natural flush.

1. Apply a light liquid or cream foundation. Blend well.

2. Use a light, shimmery eye shadow from lash line to brow.

3. With a windshield-wiper motion, apply a soft shimmery brown shadow in the crease of your eye.

4. Apply dark-brown eyeliner, using the technique on page 48.

5. Brush a soft-brown eye shadow underneath your bottom lashes.

6. Apply two coats of mascara on the top lashes and one coat on the bottom.

7. Use pink blush on the apples of the cheeks.

8. Go with a soft baby-pink (kissable!) lipstick.

chapter

10

It Takes Only One Person to Change Your Life

I T WAS 1996, AND I WAS A LITTLE BABY MAKEUP ARTIST. I KNEW I needed an agent to fight for me if I wanted to get ahead in this cutthroat business. I had tried to solicit representation from small agencies, and every door had slammed in my face. Everyone told me, "You don't have enough tear sheets." (A tear sheet is a page torn out of a magazine, on which your work appears.) I'd say, "Well, in order to get more tear sheets I need an agent, and in order to get an agent I need more tear sheets." WTF?! I was stuck between a rock and a hard place.

One day I went to a shoot for a fitness magazine (a gig I had gotten for myself through sheer hustle). I immediately fell in love with the effervescent and talented hairstylist on the shoot, Jim Crawford.

"Darling, why don't you have an agent? You are so good!" he asked me.

"Hmph! Don't even go there, Miss Thing," I said. "I've been busting my butt trying to get one, and everyone says I don't have enough work to show them."

"I'll call my agent and get you an appointment."

"Really? Get out of town! Who's your agent?"

"Jim Indorato."

I immediately started laughing. The legendary Jim Indorato, who represented the biggest, most sought-after hair and makeup artists? Whose clients regularly worked on the cover shoots for *Vogue* and *Allure*? Sure!

Fade in to me standing outside Jim Indorato's office door. I had my book and my look. Getting ready for the meeting, I had thought: *Should I show him what I can do? Maybe glitter!* There was a cool look I'd seen in *Vogue* that Irving Penn shot on Shalom Harlow; she was wearing a Philip Treacy hat and black lipstick. The height of chic. Nah, it would seem as if I was trying too hard. Maybe I should just appear businesslike. In the end, I went with a natural-ish look and a smoky eye, which would show him I was professional but a little edgy too!

Standing outside his office, I was literally shaking. I glanced up and spoke to my mom, as I had done so many times before in moments when I was terrified. "Oh, Mommy, please don't let this be as painful as I think it's going to be."

I took a big deep breath, opened the door, and walked in. At the far end of a very long room, a handsome, dark-haired man sat at a giant desk with six phones. It looked as if he was on all of them at the same time.

"Uh-huhh . . . ummm, nooo. His rate is twelve thousand dollars a day. No less!" He had a big booming voice. "Okay . . . yes, you know she flies only in first. Yes, she likes British Airways. Only."

Wow, he was FIERCE!

He didn't even look up. He just pointed to the chair in front of his desk. I sat down and placed my pathetic portfolio in front of him.

"Okay . . . sure. Oh, hi! Yes, cover of *Allure,* cover of *InStyle,* music video . . . It's all taken care of. I'll make sure he's where he needs to be. Thanks."

He hung up all the phones and took a deep breath. "Okay, who are you?"

"I'm Mally. Jim Crawford sent me. . . ."

He started flipping through my book. Fast. Barely looking. I realized that this was probably not going my way. So I took a big inhale and just let go:

"Okay, I know that my book isn't very good—I mean, I know that I don't have a ton of tear sheets, but I *really* know that I can do this. I know that you are the best and I know that it is kind of crazy that I'm sitting here right now, but I will say this: I *love* doing makeup with all my heart and I will do *anything* to work. ANYTHING. I will do whatever you say, no questions asked. If you say, 'Jump,' I'll say, 'How high?' I will work for free, I will give you all I have, and I promise I will never let you down!" It all came out in one big breath.

Halfway through my passionate plea, Jim stopped mid page-flip and stared at me.

"Are you done?" he asked.

"Yes."

Oh, crap.

He finished flipping and slammed the book shut.

"Okay. Your book is shit."

I started to stand up, the too-familiar feeling of disappointment in the pit of my stomach, and reached for my portfolio. Jim put his hand on top of it and said, "But . . ."

I slowly sat back down.

"Here's the deal: I have nothing to work with here. Basically, I'm just going to dump it." He threw the book in the trash. *Oh, my.* "But [sigh] I don't know—there's something about you. I can't really explain it. I don't know why I'm about to say this—because I've never said this before— but for some reason my gut is telling me you're a star. And I'm going to take you on."

> **"If you say, 'Jump,' I'll say, 'How high?' I will work for free, I will give you all I have, and I promise I will never let you down!"**

I couldn't believe my ears. My mouth fell open and nothing came out (for once).

"So, here's the plan. I am going to sell you over the phone. You do everything I say: no questions, no arguments. You show up on time for every job, you make me look good, and, honey, we'll go all the way to the top."

We'll go all the way to the top? *We?*

I screamed, jumped out of the chair, and fell to the ground, kicking and laughing. When I opened my eyes, I saw Jim standing up over his desk, looking at me and holding back a smile. "Don't make me change my mind."

The first to believe!

That was eighteen years ago, and Jim is still my agent. And he is also my daughter Vivienne's godfather.

And you know what? I did exactly what Jim told me to do, every single job: big jobs, little jobs. I did a gig for *American Baby* magazine. Babies? Whatever! I started out doing models and fashion, but Jimmy had real vision. He saw that celebrities were going to take over the magazine covers and editorial pages, and those were the gigs he started to get for me. The jobs got bigger and better, and the celebrities got bigger and better, and so did my book. He did everything he promised to do, and so did I.

Before I walked into Jim's office that fateful day, everyone had said no. I never gave up, though; I knew somewhere, someone would be willing to open the door for me. It took only one person to say yes.

WHEN OPPORTUNITY KNOCKS, OPEN THE DAMN DOOR!

There are things that Filipinos are famous for, some *amazing* (being kind, funny, spiritual, nurturing, and welcoming) and some that are not so great, like being late for everything. I have always made it my mission *not* to be late, as it's one of my biggest pet peeves. I see it as being disrespectful. Like, sorry, my time is more important than yours, so I'll show up when I want. Not only did I always try to be on time for jobs, I always tried to be *early*. And this time, being early really paid off.

I was young, just starting to get the fun jobs where I got to fly to locations. This morning it was only me, my makeup bag, the security guard, and some loud crickets in the lobby of Harpo Studios. I was there to do makeovers for *The Oprah Winfrey Show,* under the direction of the fabulous Mikki Taylor, who was the beauty director of *Essence* magazine at the time. "Darling, it is going to be divine!" she'd said to me. "The ladies are beautiful, and you will just be gilding the lily!" Mikki herself is one of those inspirational, delicious ladies who simply oozes elegance. Obviously, I had jumped at the chance. To have the opportunity to work with Mikki *and* be in the legendary Harpo Studios? Duh!

I stood there leaning against the wall, awake and ready to go but certainly aware that it was still dark outside. Most people in Chicago were still in REM sleep; maybe I should just go into meditation mode, I thought, and store up my energy.

Then I heard something that shook me out of my zone.

"Okay, yes! Thank you! C'mon, everyone! Let's go!"

I saw a pack of dogs come running out of a doorway. They were fast and loud and jingly. My heart started to pound, because I knew what mouth that voice was coming out of. Then there she was. Walking fast, you know, that Oprah Walk, and talking that Oprah Talk. Seriously, she could have been speaking Chinese, I couldn't tell you; all I know is that the Legend was walking up the stairs right past me.

You know that feeling you get when you're lying in bed or riding the bus and you start second-guessing something you did? You know, the woulda-shoulda-coulda moments? Yeah, I don't like that. Never did.

I took a big old breath and started talking. Never mind that I was speaking to the back of her head.

"Hello, Ms. Winfrey, my name is Mally Roncal, and I just want to let you know that you are my inspiration! I want you to know that every day I strive to be like you. I believe that God put me on this earth with a plan. I mean, when I look at you and all that you've done and created, I mean, oh my gosh, what a legacy you have! And how you help people every day! You're a communicator and I'm a communicator; I mean obviously you're much MORE of a communicator, but I try too—you know, in my own little world. Right now I'm a makeup artist, and that's my passion, but I also believe that I have a message and a mission to help, encourage, and educate people, and I just really want to stay focused and do a good job. . . ."

Halfway through my speech (which I certainly hadn't planned), Oprah slowly turned around. She looked down at me from the stairs, crossed her arms, and leaned against the banister. I stopped talking, and she said, "Are you done?"

I thought I might throw up.

"Yes. Thank you."

"Something tells me that you are going to make it," she said, and turned away, leading her dogs up the stairs and down the hall.

Seriously, you could have knocked me over with a feather! (Do people still say that?)

OPRAH just said that I was going to make it.

Now, Oprah did not know me. She didn't sit with me for three hours and hear my business plan. All she got was an earful of cray cray from this loud Filipina girl standing in her lobby before the sun had even come up. But what she did for me was priceless: She gave me fuel. Those ten words gave me permission to live my dream. They made me believe that it could happen.

So what I'm telling you is this:

When the little devil on your shoulder says, "Don't," or "You can't," ignore her. I know I've said it a million times before, but I can't say it enough: We only have one life. In the end we only regret the chances we didn't take.

The I-Mean-Business Face

To make a good impression, you need to make a little effort. A 2011 scientific study confirmed that not only does wearing the right makeup make a woman feel more confident but also that other people will perceive her as more confident, competent, and in charge. Here's a strong but subtle look that will tell everyone that you are not messing around! I'd describe it as natural with a shot of fierce.

1. Apply your foundation: You want a blemish-free, satiny finish.

2. Highlight your cheekbones. With the Cinnamon Bun Method, swirl a soft-peachy blush with a little shimmer onto the apples of your cheeks.

3. Apply shadow base from lash line to brow, then a nude shadow (maybe with a tiny bit of shimmer) from lash line to brow.

4. Blend a deep matte (but not flat) brown shadow up to the crease of the eye in a windshield-wiper motion.

5. Using the same dark-brown shadow, line the lower lashes and smudge to soften.

6. Thinly line the upper lash line with a sharp black pencil. Soften the line with your finger or a brush.

7. With your finger or a brush dipped in the nude shadow, tap the center of your eyelid to make your eyes look bigger and brighter.

8. Brush two coats of mascara onto your upper lashes and one coat onto your bottom lashes.

9. Add contour to the hollows of your cheeks (see page 132).

10. Finish with a nude lipstick slicked with a tiny bit of gloss.

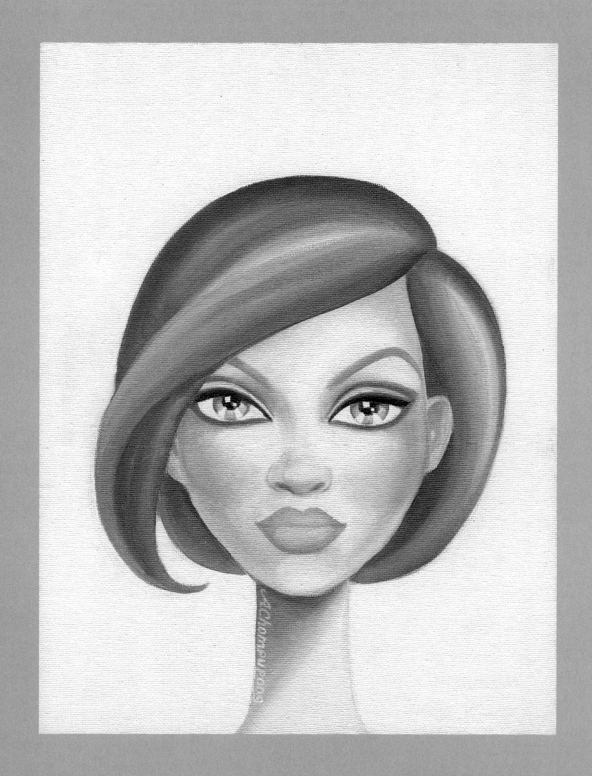

chapter

11

Be Fierce,
Be Free,
Be Fearless

EVERYTHING WAS SO GOOD. I WAS A YOUNG MAKEUP ARTIST on the cusp of great things. I had the best agent in the world. I was hungry and willing to take any job.

One day, my agent, Jim, called to tell me that I was going to do a cover and fashion story for a top magazine. Better yet, I was going to be shooting with a major photographer, a hot hairstylist, and a hotter supermodel.

I showed up at work in Mally drag du jour: platinum-blond hair, aqua-green smoky eyes, false lashes, pastel-pink lipstick—the usual—and was introduced to the team. Even though it was obvious that they had worked together before (usually the photographer finds a stylist, hairstylist, and makeup artist he or she likes and uses them over and over), everyone made me feel really welcome and comfortable.

When you shoot on location, it's always an adventure. We were headed to an abandoned mansion in the middle of the woods in Upstate New York. We drove up in a big, not very stable motor home, bagels and coffee and juice flying everywhere as we bounced down the road. There's something about being on location that makes everyone let their guard down. You're all working toward a common goal of creating a beautiful picture, and you bond with the people you work with pretty quickly, no matter how *fabulous* they are. Well, most of the time.

We had a great day. The model was perfect, her hair was exquisite, the styling was inspired, the photos were incredible, and I can humbly say that the makeup was some of the best I had ever done to date.

I was feeling confident and happy—invincible!

We all laughed and carried on during the ride home, and when we got back into the city I hugged everyone goodbye and thanked them for this life-changing experience. "See you next time! Thank you so much!"

I had brand-new besties, and, oh, did I mention that they also happened to be the coolest kids in town?

I was about to leave, when the hairstylist said, "Can we talk?"

I just knew he was going to ask me to hang out over the weekend, or, better yet, maybe he wanted me to be his new makeup partner!

"Can I give you a little advice?"

> *"Honey, if you want to be taken seriously as a makeup artist, you've got to drop this shtick."*

"Yes, please!" I've always been the kind of person who welcomes constructive criticism.

"Okay, your makeup was really good. And you're *so* sweet and you have great energy. Everyone really loved you."

I was grinning from ear to ear. I had been so nervous at first and wanted to do a great job and have everyone accept me, and I had done it!

"But . . ."

But?

"This thing you are doing . . ." he said, as he waved his hand at me from head to toe. "Honey, if you want to be taken seriously as a makeup artist, you've got to drop this shtick. The hair, the lashes, the platforms—I mean, honey, we were in the country!" Okay, maybe he had a point, but heels were as comfortable for me as running shoes! "All I can say is, look at all the big players, the makeup stars:

They don't even wear makeup! Don't you want to be like them? Because, if you do, you have to try to be taken seriously as a real artist. And you have to look the part. Honey, I hate to tell you, but you look ridiculous. Everybody thought you did great work, but, if you want to know the truth, they were laughing at you."

My heart sank. Laughing at me? Did I really look that bad? The way I looked was my art, my way of expressing myself. I was my own work in progress, and I was searching for ways to show the world who I was, not only with my talent but with my style.

Me in my Daisy Dukes with my beautiful Aunties

When I got home, Phil had gotten in just ahead of me.

"How was it?" he asked as he gave me a hug. He had been as excited about the assignment as I was.

When we pulled back, he saw that I was crying.

"They were laughing at me." I could barely get the words out.

"What? Why? Was the makeup bad?"

"No, they loved the makeup. It was *me*. They said that I looked ridiculous and that if I wanted to be taken seriously I would have to look like everyone else."

"Are you f***ing kidding me?" Phil yelled. "That is the dumbest thing I have ever heard! Forget those people, Mally! They don't deserve you, your love, *or* your talent!"

I know that Phil was angry because he loves me any way I am, but I couldn't help but think that maybe that hairdresser was right.

A couple of days later I had another job, and I decided to take the hairstylist's advice.

I showed up very un-Mally-like, with my hair in a low pony, no makeup, jeans, a white tank, and flip-flops. I walked into the studio and introduced myself—hello to the photographer, hi to the hair guy, hey to the stylist and model. No pizzazz, no love, no Mally.

On shoots, I was usually the one standing behind the photographer, doing high kicks and trying to make the model laugh. I was the one making up the craft-services chick on our downtime or letting the hairstylist who was looking for inspiration for his next test-shoot experiment on me. I used my days at work not just to create beautiful makeup but to share love, laughter, and joy with everyone I worked with. My look was a part of who I was; today, it was as if part of me was missing, and I hated the way I felt.

I met Phil at a sushi restaurant after work. As soon as I sat down, I let out everything I'd been feeling.

> **"If people can't love me for who I am and for what I bring to the table, then you know what? I'll go where I am appreciated!"**

"You were right! You know what? Forget those people! I don't care what they say! I don't care if I ever am a 'star.'" And, yes, I did the finger quotes here! "I don't care where I'm doing makeup. I love it and I will do it anywhere. And I am *me*. If people can't love me for who I am and for what I bring to the table, then you know what? I'll go where I am appreciated!" And I gave three finger snaps in a big Z.

On my job the next day, I went for it. BIG hair, BIG lashes, BIG smoky eyes, and the BIGGEST heels I had.

I felt great. I did beautiful makeup that I was proud of. I hugged everyone (and I didn't care if it wasn't cool), laughed as loud as I could, and, yes, my crazy high kicks had the model cracking up!

I had the best day ever. And so did the photographer. At the end of it he said, "You know what? You're awesome! I love your makeup, I love your energy, I love how you own your look! And I'm wondering—I just got my first big gig shooting the cover of a magazine next week. And I need to have you there."

I had won. By just being *me*.

So what's the moral of my story? No matter what, be true to who you are. Own who you are. Forget the haters. *Don't let them dull your shine.* What may not be right for them could be right for you. Be you, and you win every time.

Don't Play It Safe!

Have Fun with Color

Listen: I grew up in the seventies and eighties. I have no problem with blue eye shadow and frosted pink lipstick, even today. But, truth be told, there's a right way and a wrong way to wear color. Here's how to do it without looking too cray cray.

1. The more real estate you're going to cover, the sheerer the color should be. If you want to use a bright eye shadow, apply a translucent wash of color.

2. Go for it with eyeliner. After you've put on your shadow, instead of using a neutral color, line your eyes with green, violet, teal, or aqua (or any color!), drawing a line from the outer to the inner corner of the eye. Finish with two coats of mascara on the top lashes and one coat on the bottom.

3. Alternatively, keep your eyes natural and bring the focus to your lips with a pop of bright red, pink, or fuchsia. Put it on straight from the tube and blot. If this sounds too bold for you, try a vivid color with a sheer finish.

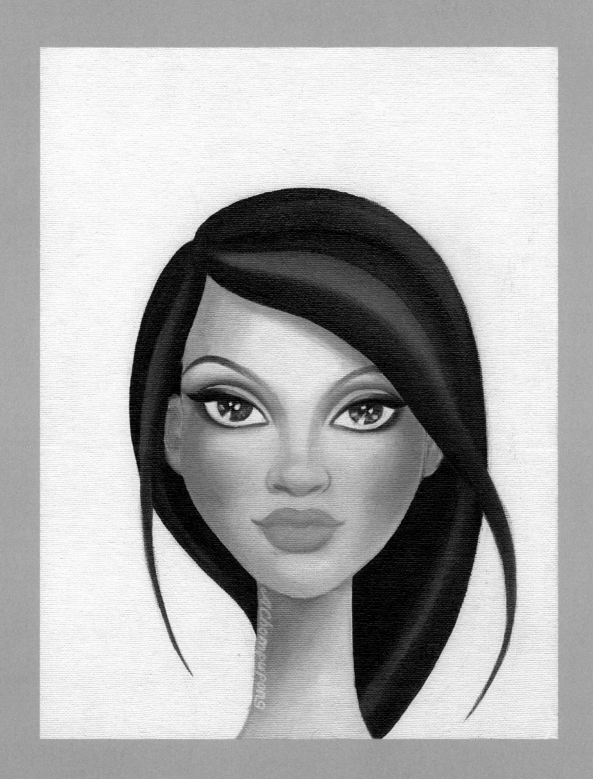

Rock False Eyelashes

Let's talk about some false eyelashes. It's one of the biggest makeup mysteries, because we all know that they can make your eyes look bigger and flirtier, but they're hard to put on *and* to pull off. I'm going to make this simple for you, with instructions for daytime lashes and all-out nighttime glamour lashes.

INDIVIDUAL LASHES

1. Curl your natural lashes.

2. Lay out your individuals on a clean hard surface.

3. Squeeze a small puddle of glue onto the back of your nondominant hand, pick up a lash with a tweezer, and dip one end into the glue. Give the glue a second to get tacky.

4. Then, looking down in a mirror, take the individual lash and place it gently as close and as deep down between your lashes as possible.

5. Repeat until you feel your lashes are as full as you would like them to look.

6. Marry the false lashes to your own with two coats of mascara. Pro trick: Leave the tips of the lashes free from mascara; they'll look more feathery.

STRIP LASHES

1. Curl your natural lashes.

2. Apply one coat of mascara.

3. Put glue along the whole strip of the lashes and give it a second to get tacky.

4. Looking down into a mirror, gently press the lashes down against your own lash line.

5. Seal the deal with a coat of mascara.

Be Sparkly!

Glitter isn't just for drag queens or little girls playing dress-up. There's a way to wear it—yes, *every* day—that looks fresh and pretty. You can always amp up the volume for a night out.

1. Apply your regular makeup. A glittery accent works especially well with a soft or a smoky eye.

2. You'll need something clear, with a little texture and an emollient quality that isn't too greasy or sticky, on which to apply the glitter. I used to use a clear lip gloss; now I use a luminizer cream. Tap the product either from your eyelashes to your creases or from just above your eyeliner to the creases.

3. Dip your pinky or a small brush into the glitter and press it onto the product on your lid and the inner corner of your eye; it should adhere pretty easily.

4. If you have any drippage, wrap some adhesive tape (it's a drag queen's best friend) around your finger (sticky side out, of course!) and use it to pick up the rogue sparkles.

chapter

12

Trust
Your Gut

My PHONE RANG EARLY ONE AFTERNOON. IT WAS JIM.

"Get your stuff together," he said. "There's a premiere for a Mike Myers movie tonight. It's called *Goldmember,* and you're going to do Beyoncé."

This sort of "get your stuff together" call was nothing really new for me. In a freelance life, you have to be ready to go on the drop of a dime. It's totally normal to be sitting at an outdoor café having a delicious lunch when your phone rings and someone tells you that you have to leave for Paris for two weeks. Now. And you pretty much have to do it—it's work, and it's money. You have to grab the chance when you can. It may not be there tomorrow, and if you don't take it, someone else most certainly will. You could lose the opportunity of a lifetime. And this was one for me.

Of course, Beyoncé had already enjoyed incredible success as a part of the group Destiny's Child. But now she was on the cusp of Major Beyoncé Superstardom.

I showed up at the hotel, ready to go. Her assistant let me into the room, and I started to set up a makeshift makeup station in the bathroom. About twenty minutes later, I heard the door open and turned around. What I saw took my breath

The day that changed it all

away. Beyoncé was standing there in a gorgeous gold jewel-encrusted gown and bare feet, with big honey-kissed curly hair and not a stitch of makeup on her incredible face. Her skin was flawless, poreless, and the color of coffee with a little cream in it. She was much smaller than I'd imagined, almost fragile. Definitely not the Superwoman image that you see on the stage. I immediately wanted to hug her, but I didn't.

"Hi, I'm Beyoncé," she said in her famously low, smooth voice as she extended her hand to shake mine.

"Hi, I'm Mally. Wow! You're amazing!" Even her hand was flawless.

She laughed and said, "Thank you," as she sat down in front of the mirror.

My mouth was probably still hanging open as my mind started racing a million miles an hour: *I can't believe this is happening right now! Wow, she's a lot shorter than I thought—well, she's taller than me, but who isn't? And that HAIR . . . and SKIN! What am I going to do here? Hmmm . . . the dress is so formal and sparkly. Maybe I should go there. Glitter? Hmm . . . no. Smoky? Nah.*

The longer I looked at her reflection in the mirror, the more I realized one thing: She needed almost nothing.

I excused myself for a minute. I needed to think. I knew I could give her the makeup style I had seen on her many times before, but something told me to go in a completely different direction.

I took a deep breath and headed back into the bathroom, where she was waiting. Her super publicist, Yvette Noel-Schure, was there, talking with Beyoncé and looking through a stack of magazines that had her client either on the cover or in a feature. What was about to happen for Beyoncé was going to be huge, and everyone knew it.

A good makeup artist behaves like a great waiter. You are attentive and nurturing, but you can also be invisible. You can be a therapist or you can be a fly on the wall. You have to be able to work quickly and tune out all that's going on around you. You have to realize that your client and her team will be having confidential conversations in your presence, and you need to NOT hear a thing. Just do your job—unless someone asks your opinion.

I looked at Beyoncé's reflection in the mirror and knew I had to follow my gut.

So I did. And in ten minutes I was done. A little concealer, shimmery bronze shadow, two coats of mascara, and very little foundation—almost none. Lipstick? No, just sheer blue-pink gloss. Comb up those great brows. No brow pencil. And pink blush. Okay, done.

Love her so much!

I waited for a break in their conversation and then said, "Excuse me, ladies, I'm finished. Shall I wait for you out there?"

They both stopped and looked at me.

"Um . . . makeup takes two hours," Beyoncé said.

"Well, with all due respect, with your face and my makeup, it takes ten minutes." I smiled.

She gave me a look that I interpreted as "Girl, you realize that this moment could end your career, but, okay, let's do it."

I packed up my stuff, partly excited and partly nervous. We hung out for a few minutes, and then I saw her off to the premiere and jumped in a cab myself.

I called Phil immediately.

"So?" he answered.

"O. M. Geeeeeeeeee! That was AWESOME! I love her! She's soooo nice! And *gorg*! And funny! And cool!"

"Mally! How was the makeup? What did you do?"

"I just followed my gut. It took me ten minutes. I mean, she's already perfect."

"Did she like it?"

"I think so. She said she did. I guess I'll find out soon enough."

Five days later, I got a phone call from Yvette Noel-Schure. I had no idea what she was going to say.

"Hi, Mally. There were three premieres: New York, L.A., London. Three different makeup artists. We laid all the pictures out. So, she wants to know, what are you doing for the next year?"

That day changed the course of my life. Beyoncé has become a part of my heart and such a source of incredible inspiration personally, spiritually, and professionally. Since then I have had the honor and pleasure of working with her on so many projects—too many to count. From movies to videos, from photo shoots to awards shows, from TV interviews to personal appearances, I got to see the world with her on our journey. Her work ethic, her boundless energy, her humor, her beauty (inside as well as outside), her passion, her generosity, and most of all

Goldmember New York premiere, July 24, 2002

her humility are all qualities I respect and admire. Her friendship is priceless to me, and I wouldn't trade it for the world.

You see, my loves? You must trust your gut. Trust your intuition. I believe these feelings are God talking to you and leading you in the right direction. And this will never steer you wrong.

Beyoncé's Ten-Minute Face

Beyoncé is a chameleon. She's one of those women who can wear anything and make it look right. Here's what I did for her the first time we worked together. It's a perfect illustration of less being more.

1. Use a concealer to even out your skin tone. Blend well.

2. Highlight your cheekbones. Use a light hand.

3. Apply a shimmery bronzy-brown shadow from lash line to crease and under the eye.

4. Use a sharp black eyeliner pencil to create a natural line (see page 48).

5. Put a light shimmery shadow or highlighter on the inner corners of your eyes.

6. Use two coats of mascara on the top lashes and one coat on the bottom.

7. Put a pop of pinky blush on the apples of the cheeks.

8. Apply a sheer blue-pink lip gloss. You're a star, baby!

chapter

13

Jump into the Deep End

MY LIFE AS A FULL-TIME PROFESSIONAL CELEBRITY MAKEUP artist was pretty damn awesome. On any given day I could be on a private jet being whisked to Tanzania for a photo shoot, getting Kelly Osbourne ready for a photo shoot in a 7-star hotel (yes, they do exist!) in Paris, making up Zooey Deschanel for a *Paper* magazine cover or Anna Paquin or Taylor Swift for a personal appearance, or touching up a client backstage at the Grammys. It looked glamorous on paper, but I wasn't sure how much longer I could handle this kind of schedule. It was *crazy* busy. And demanding. And exhausting. For one long stretch, I basically never saw my apartment. I didn't even know what day it was or what time zone I was in. I missed Phil and wanted to start a family. I wanted to create something of my own, something unique that hadn't been done yet and that only I could do.

One day I knew it was time to make a change. I was standing in a parking lot in Los Angeles on a break during a shoot for a Mary J. Blige album cover. I called Phil.

"Remember the idea we had about starting our own makeup line? It's time."

When the job was done the next day, I flew back home and we got to work

I love QVC!

turning our idea into a reality. At the time, I was the spokesperson for Sephora. It was my job to know everything about every line out there, and while there was some amazing makeup available, there was no one line that offered everything *I* needed. My clients like Alicia Keys and Destiny's Child were performers and needed to look good under hot lights while singing, dancing, and shaking their famous booties. They needed to look fresh and beautiful day to night and under the most intense conditions.

I'd been picking and choosing products from different lines and even mixing them together in my kitchen to get the results I wanted for my clients. I needed formulas that were easy to apply, looked super-refined and polished with minimal effort, and were, as I call it, "bulletproof." I wanted products that incorporated my years of trial and error and professional tricks. That kind of magic just wasn't out there. Oh, and one more thing: *I* needed to sell it. *I* needed to be the one to communicate, to teach the consumer. My people needed me to go on the journey with them. And I was finally ready.

One thing that has been a constant in my life is that I have never done anything the way it was *supposed* to be done. I've *always* taken a different approach from the expected. As the spokesperson for Sephora, I could have launched my new makeup line with them. That would have been the obvious choice. But going that way didn't feel right. There was only *one* way that I would be able to show my customers my tips, secrets, and application techniques and sell them my product, and that was by going on TV.

When I was growing up, QVC was on all the time at our house; I've been a loyal viewer all my life. We Filipinos LOVE television shopping! In fact, it was my dad who had the idea first. "Melissa, why don't you sell your product on QBC?" he asked in his Filipino accent. Best. Idea. Ever.

We got an appointment with Michele Tacconelli, the head beauty buyer at QVC. I was so excited that I didn't even care that we had no products to show her. I believed so much in our idea that I knew I could sell it to her even though it was all on paper and in our hearts.

> *"Hang on to your hats. I just met the next big thing!"*

Phil and I sat around a conference table at QVC headquarters, armed and ready with our PowerPoint presentation, VHS tape, props, and books. We were really going to wow her!

We began by talking about who we were, who I was, my celebrity clients, and the idea behind Mally Beauty. Then we popped in the tape of my many TV appearances. It was kind of long, and I noticed that Michele was starting to thumb through our deck of PowerPoint slides. Oh, *shit!* We were starting to lose her. I had to do something. And *fast.*

I grabbed the remote, stopped the tape, jumped up on the conference table, and planted my butt right down in front of her. I know I totally startled her, but I needed her to hear me.

"Okay, so here's the deal—I *love* QVC! And I *love* makeup. I've been doing this for a long time, and there is *nothing* I love more than teaching women how to look and feel fierce. Now, I know that we don't have a line. We don't even have one product to show you, but I will tell you this: If you say that we can do this together, I will show you that we will not only make the BEST product on the market that you have ever seen, but we will entertain and educate your customer like she's never been entertained and educated before. You *need* to buy this line from me and you need to buy it *right now,* because if you don't, it's never going to be. I'm not launching it anywhere else."

I held my breath as I looked into Michele's eyes.

"Have you ever been here at QVC?" she asked after a ten-second pause. "Let me give you a tour."

And the meeting that was supposed to last ten minutes lasted two hours.

Later, when Mally Beauty was blessed with success, Michele told me that after our initial meeting she went back to her office and told her assistant, "Hang on to your hats. I just met the next big thing!"

Dreams come true!

The Sculpted Face

Want to look like you just lost five pounds without giving up carbs? Good news: Contouring has come a long way since the eighties. I'm sharing my secrets so you can have the cheekbones and jawline you wish you'd been born with. You can use any texture product you like. Professionals often use creams; you can certainly use powder. I do all the time. Now pass the bagels and grab a brush.

1. Take a powder or cream highlighter or concealer and apply it gently on your cheekbones, starting right under your temple. Now apply your highlighter or concealer between your brows, down the center of your nose, on your chin, and on the Cupid's bow of your lips.

2. Swirl a brush into a contouring powder or a deeper shade of foundation, and if you're using powder shake off the excess. Apply it on your temples first, then make a fish face and apply in the hollows you made when you sucked in your cheeks. Now, starting behind your ear, sweep the brush down across your jawline to the tip of your chin and repeat on the other side of your face. Softly blend down to your neck so there's no obvious line. Blend, blend, blend!

3. Apply blush to the apples of your cheeks, using the Cinnamon Bun Method (see page 50).

chapter

14

Share Your Love and Wisdom

ONE OF THE MANY THINGS I LOVE ABOUT WHAT I DO IS teaching and nurturing young talent. Some of my assistants have gone on to great careers on their own; others have grown into roles working for me and Mally Beauty. Teenie's story is one of my favorites.

In 2004 I was looking for a new assistant and called around to friends and colleagues for leads. One of my best childhood friends, Virginia, said, "I think I know the perfect person for you. Her name is Christine Fulwiler." I asked her to have Christine call me and set up an appointment to meet Phil and me at our little one-bedroom Greenwich Village apartment, which was both home and home base for my business.

Teenie makes me so proud!

When the doorbell rang, I opened the door with our two rescue dogs—G-Love, a chocolate Lab mix, and Bingka (named after a very sweet Filipino dessert), a pit-bull–whippet mix—at my side. There stood a very pretty young woman with a slicked-back ponytail, big hoop earrings, and pale frosted lipstick outlined in dark lip liner. When she saw the dogs, she backed up until she hit the opposite wall, fear in her eyes. Let me say that when you're looking for an assistant, terror is *not* something you want to see at your first meeting.

Phil put the dogs in the bedroom, and I was finally able to coax her inside. She calmed down and introduced herself.

I explained that I was looking for someone to be both my personal assistant and my makeup assistant. She would work with me in my home office when I wasn't on a shoot and would accompany me when I was. I would teach her everything I knew. She'd have the opportunity to travel around the world and work with A-list celebrities.

Most people who applied for the job would have said, "Absolutely!" and jumped at the chance. Teenie just sat there and stared at me like the proverbial deer in the headlights.

I certainly didn't want to force her to do something she didn't want to, but I trusted Virginia's judgment and I had a gut feeling that, behind all the fear and insecurity, there was a strong and determined woman just dying to be let out.

"You can do this!" I told her, and reluctantly she said, "Okay . . ."

"Good. You start tomorrow."

Before I met Teenie, I had never met anyone who was afraid of so many things: dogs, sleeping away from home, flying, certain foods, anything new or unknown or unfamiliar. Our first assignment together was working with Mariah Carey at her home. It was the biggest apartment I'd ever seen—very elegant, very feminine, very opulent. There was a lot of white—white marble floors and carpet, plush white upholstery, a white baby grand piano, and beautiful flowers and candles burning everywhere. There were clothes and shoe rooms (they were too big to be called closets) and even a fully outfitted exercise room, something you don't usually see in a New York apartment. I was used to working with celebrities in this kind of setting, but I had to pick Teenie's jaw up off the floor. She pulled it together and did a great job, and we both breathed a sigh of relief afterward.

In 2005, we had a gig I knew was really going to test Teenie. We flew to California to work on the video for the Destiny's Child single "Cater 2 U." I was doing Beyoncé's makeup for a segment that would be shot on location in the desert, when I got called away to do Kelly Rowland's makeup on the main set.

I looked into Teenie's eyes and took both her hands in mine.

"Remember the story I told you about how I learned to swim? How my dad threw me into the deep end of the pool? Well, you're about to go swimming. You can do this; I believe in you."

She looked at me, panicked. "I *can't!*"

"You *can,* and you *will,*" I said, and handed her the lip gloss and set bag (which contained everything she would need for a makeup emergency), wished her luck, and drove off.

An hour later, the door to the motor home that was serving as makeup central for the shoot opened, and in walked Beyoncé (looking gorgeous), followed by Teenie, wearing the biggest smile I'd ever seen.

She walked over to me and said, "I did it!" and we high-fived.

That day was the beginning of an amazing transformation. Sparked by that tiny bit of confidence, Teenie, who has a real talent for organization and planning, took charge of managing our QVC shows, as well as all of our shoots

> **"Sometimes a person can't see the light they shine, and they need someone else to turn on the switch."**

and my personal appearances. Sometimes her belief in herself wavered and she tried to quit, but I wouldn't let her. She'd come so far that I couldn't let her give up.

Today, Teenie is a star in her own right. She's the face of Mally Beauty for QVC Italy and Germany, goes on air with me on QVC U.K., and represents

Backstage at Fashion Week

Mally Beauty on QVC America if I can't be there. She's growing her dreams and aspirations and surprises herself (but not me!) every day. She's from Brooklyn, and when she gets her back up or when someone tries to mess with me, her Brooklyn side comes out—it's a real change from the shy, scared girl that I first met! And, by the way, she now has two dogs of her own.

Sometimes a person can't see the light they shine, and they need someone else to turn on the switch. I was able to do it for Teenie, and now it's her turn to do it for someone else. Saying thank you for the good things in your life isn't enough; we all need to pay it forward. When I'm at the airport I've even been known to stop a woman walking to her gate and redo her makeup or work on her brows! If you've been given a gift—time, money, talent—share it. It's simply the right thing to do, and I've always found I get back far more than I give. What may not seem like a big deal to you may be just enough to change someone else's life.

Sharing the love. Go Team Mally!

Bright, Beautiful Eyes

I love discovering new talent, and I love seeing the world with the same wide-eyed optimism and enthusiasm. You can have that wide-eyed look too.

1. Apply eye shadow base from lash line to brow.

2. Brush a shimmery champagne shadow from lash line to brow.

3. Smudge a matte blond shadow into the crease and along the bottom lash line.

4. Draw a very thin line of black liner on the top lash line.

5. With your finger or a brush, tap more champagne shadow on the center of your top lid and onto the inner corners of your eyes.

6. Finish with two coats of mascara on the top lashes and one on the bottom lashes.

chapter

15

Demand the Best

I WORKED WITH JENNIFER LOPEZ FOR THE FIRST TIME IN 2004, when she launched her first perfume, Glow. She walked into the room in a white bathrobe, no makeup, and wet hair, and I was starstruck. Working with her made me realize that when you're confident you can wear *any* look, even if all you're wearing is a bathrobe.

Being in Jennifer's presence can be a little intimidating at first, because she just radiates confidence; that girl does *not* need to fake it. She looks at you as if she's saying, "I do all I can to be at the top of my game, and I expect the same from you." That's not only motivating, it's inspiring, and I've tried to instill that in my team too.

Another thing I love about working with Jennifer is how much she enjoys the process. Every session is crazy luxurious, with candles and big fluffy white towels everywhere. She always blocks out plenty of time so nothing is rushed. I could spend an hour on her lashes alone, even though if I had to, I could get her face done in ten minutes in a moving car! We should all take a lesson from Jennifer. We women slap on our makeup and throw on a pair of jeans and run out the door. Why don't we find that time to appreciate what we do for *ourselves*? We

The Best!

deserve it! Take those extra few minutes in the morning; when we breathe and enjoy the process of getting ourselves together, we honor ourselves. Creating that space can change your frequency for the rest of the day.

Jennifer is so smart and so aware. She knows what's going on in the business, and she knows what's going on on the other side of the room. For example, she loves freshly baked chocolate chip cookies. One time, we were in the middle of a session and someone handed her a plate with two cookies. She took a bite and said, "Those aren't fresh baked. They're regular cookies that you put in the microwave." Now *that's* attention to detail!

When you demand the best, it doesn't have to be about the most expensive face cream or a reservation at the hottest restaurant. Demanding the best is about knowing how you value yourself. Too often we put others before ourselves.

I know I do it; I always make sure that my family is taken care of before I take care of myself. Let's try to change it up. What makes you feel good? Is it a luxurious, hot scented bath? A long, solitary walk in the park? A massage or a facial? Sneaking away to T.J.Maxx for an hour? Make it happen. You need it, and you're worth it.

Glow Like JLo

Bronzer How-To

Using bronzer can be dicey; if you do it wrong, you can wind up looking . . . well, dirty! Be sure to use a matte bronzer a shade or two deeper than your skin tone.

1. Start behind the back of your ear and come down the jawline; that way, if there's too much color on the brush, it won't be as noticeable. Go all around the perimeter of your face. The biggest mistake we make is that we go all over the face with bronzer. It looks flat and super-fake!

2. Apply a light swipe of bronzer across your forehead, the apples of your cheeks, and chin.

3. Add highlighter only to cheekbones, the tip of your nose, and the Cupid's bow of your lip.

4. Finally, smile and add a pop of sheer pink to the apples of cheeks and the tops of your eyebrows to simulate that "burn" from the sun. Looks believable!

The Perfect Nude Lip

1. Make sure your lips are exfoliated and smooth. Apply lip balm and let it sink in.

2. Apply a nude lipstick with a hint of pink or peach. (If you wear a pink blush, go for pink; if you wear a peach blush, go peachy.) Make sure it has some color so it doesn't look like concealer (and you don't look dead!).

3. Subtly line your lips with a lip liner a TINY bit deeper than your natural lip color. This adds definition.

4. Apply a nude gloss in the center of your bottom and top lips to give them dimension and life.

chapter

16

What Is Your "All"?

P HIL AND I WERE READY TO HAVE KIDS, AND, LIKE SO MANY couples, we discovered we needed help. We were so fortunate; in 2006, I became pregnant with twins. After we saw them on the first ultrasound, we called them the Beans (and we still do), because they looked like two little peas in a pod.

The babies were growing and healthy throughout my first trimester, and I was nauseated pretty much 24/7. It was like being the drunkest, dizziest you've ever been but not being able to throw up. The *worst*. When the beans got bigger, I had sciatic nerve pain, but as long as the babies were doing well, I could deal.

I worked throughout my pregnancy. In October, I had an early call time for our last big set of QVC shows before I went on maternity leave. Phil, our team, and I were staying at a hotel the night before the first show. The Beans still had plenty of time to cook; I wasn't due until mid-January. But in the middle of the night I began to feel cramping in my tummy, throbbing in my thighs, and pressure in my vagina.

I shook Phil awake, and within minutes the hotel manager was giving us a high-speed escort to the nearest emergency room, where a young blond doctor examined me.

"How are you feeling? Does it hurt? Don't worry, we are going to take care of you and the babies," she said.

Tears were streaming down my cheeks. I had never been so afraid in my life.

"I can feel the baby's head," the doctor turned to Phil and said. "You need to get her out of here. This hospital is not equipped to deal with two premature babies of this size. How fast can you get her back to her doctor and hospital?"

Long (and terrifying) story short, they gave me drugs to slow down the contractions and I made it to my hospital safely, praying silently the whole way.

I had to spend several days in the hospital, until the doctors were sure my premature labor was under control. For the first time ever, I missed appearing on a Mally Beauty QVC show, but I called in to speak on air. I felt so much love from the QVC community and our Mallynistas. They all said, "Don't worry, Mally, we'll be here when you get back. Just go make those beautiful babies."

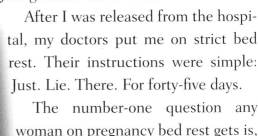

After I was released from the hospital, my doctors put me on strict bed rest. Their instructions were simple: Just. Lie. There. For forty-five days.

The number-one question any woman on pregnancy bed rest gets is, "Didn't you go crazy?" The truth is, I did not. Lying there in our king-size bed with a giant U-shaped body pillow, attached to a monitor to measure any contractions, with a needle in my thigh for the IV drugs to control those contractions, I found this place of peace, this place of Zen. I felt as if I had truly found my reason for living. I had done so much in my life that I thought was so important, but you know what?

Zen Mama

That was nothing compared to just being. It wasn't about me; it was about growing these babies. I talked to them, I sang to them, I ate and drank for them. I couldn't wait to meet them.

Worked 'til the end!

In December 2006, Pilar Elizabeth and Sophie Grace were born, one month early and kind of puny, but happy and healthy. Our lives were complete. Or at least we thought so until November 2009, when Vivienne was born. Then we knew what true and utter contentment was.

There was only one thing I missed from my pre-baby life: those luxurious moments hanging out in front of the mirror, getting my hair and makeup *just so*. For a while, I had to kiss those times goodbye.

After my Beans came into my life, my looks changed so quickly it made my head spin. My long thick hair, which had gotten extra full when I was pregnant, started falling out by the handful. My face was as round as the moon. When I was breast-feeding, my boobs were bigger than my head. My skin was dry and flaky, because I didn't have a second to moisturize. And why didn't anyone tell me that extra baby weight doesn't just fall off after you give birth? That's rude!

Who *was* this person in the mirror?

I was tired and overwhelmed, but a few months after the Beans were born, I decided it was time to say goodbye to the flabby, pale, alligator-skinned, sour-milk-scented version of me. I started with my big, round, full, bloated face. Sleepless nights along with hormones that had attacked like ninjas, out of nowhere, were to blame for the two puffy slits where my eyes used to be. I needed big guns. I pulled out my City Chick Smokey Eye Kit and said, "Okay, honey, it's you and me." And you know what? Every day from then on, I rocked a smoky eye like a drag queen at the Gay Pride Parade. I was lucky enough that I knew how to slap it on in a heartbeat; I remember doing it one time when Pilar was attached to my boob (my girlfriend said, "Now, that's talent!"). Putting on that smoky eye made me feel slightly in control. It made me feel pretty. It made me feel like myself, when I didn't really even know who "myself" was anymore.

When we went to Target, I would push our double stroller down the aisles and women would stop me. "Awwww, twins! God bless you! But, wow, you look great! Good for you for doing your face!" I was proud. I felt as if I was showing the world that I still cared.

So to all the fierce mamas out there: Just because we've had babies doesn't mean we're destined to wear sweatpants and baggy T-shirts forever. Take your time to figure out who you were before, who you are now, and who you want to be. Inside every mother is a sexy mama. She deserves to be celebrated. I'm forty-two, with three little girls, and I *refuse* to let go of my smoky-eyed self. I made a vow to get in the best shape of my life and feel like the most beautiful version of me, and I'm still working hard to get there. I'm kind to myself, though. I eat the fries, but then I work hard at barre class or Pilates to make up for it. I try to get

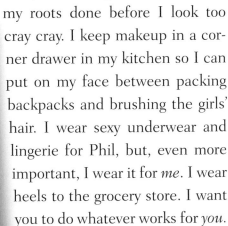

my roots done before I look too cray cray. I keep makeup in a corner drawer in my kitchen so I can put on my face between packing backpacks and brushing the girls' hair. I wear sexy underwear and lingerie for Phil, but, even more important, I wear it for *me*. I wear heels to the grocery store. I want you to do whatever works for *you*.

As the girls grow and thrive, I continue to learn so much about myself as a mother and a person.

Smoky eye Mom!

They've changed me in so many ways. First of all, I now know what true selfless-ness is. Had a busy day? Crazy things going on at work? Friends or extended fam-ily making you nuts? Really, you want to take a shower? Or maybe take a dump without an audience? Oh, are you just TIRED? Babies come first! It's my job to tend to their every need. And those needs change from age to age, from diapers to ballet tutus, from baby food to bagels, from dealing with colic to dealing with a kid slapping a pizza slice out of your child's hand in the lunchroom. Their needs are your needs; their problems are your problems; their successes and joys are yours. Let's be honest—there are days when it seems impossible to be the parent you feel or think you should be. But it's our job to try to be the best we can for them.

SO MANY PEOPLE LOOK at my life and ask, "How do you do it? What's the secret to having it all?"

And I tell them that it depends on what your "all" is, and that it changes de-pending on where you are in your life. When I was in my early twenties, my all was finding a job or career I loved and having best friends who accepted and celebrated me for who I was—blue eye shadow, false eyelashes, everything. Later in my twenties and my early thirties, it was rocking hard on my career and building my artistic reputation while nurturing my relationship with my new husband.

And now? My all is having a family I adore and being a wife and mommy first, but it's just as important to me to touch and inspire people, and to lead a brand that helps them look and feel amazing. I'm so fortunate to be able to work with my husband at my side. We work hard, we play hard, we love with all our hearts. It may not be for everyone, but it works for us. You know, some-one once said that working hard for something you don't care about is called stress, but working hard for something you care about is called passion. I want to have a husband and family who know that they are first in my life, but they also know that in order to be a whole human, I need to be able to do my job with passion.

Nobody makes me laugh like my babies.

Playing in the dirt

My kids = my heart

Viv's first day home. Pilar asked, "Can we keep her?"

I've also found that it's the little things that make me happiest—they truly are greater than the sum of their parts. Some of mine are: lunch duty at my daughters' school once a week (I get to see my babies out in the world, and it's fun when they forget that I'm coming and run to give me a hug); barre class (it clears my mind and keeps my ass from falling); massages (the only time I can really relax); cooking Filipino food (my connection to who I am); a healthy and happy marriage with Phil (including lots of sex, which, yes, we have several times a week. It fulfills us both on many levels, from physical to spiritual—I know, corny!).

That's my all today, and, yes, I am proud to say I have it. Today.

The question you have to ask yourself is: What is *your* all? What do *you* want? What

Pure love

will fulfill *you* as a human being? Is it being a businessperson who can have a family too? Is it being a stay-at-home mom who devotes herself to her family and community? Is it being a hip city chick with a blog and a tech day job, dating lots of different people? Are you ready to leave the nine-to-five world and follow your bliss?

Forget what everyone else says. Put what you want into words. Say it out loud. Say it often. Say it to yourself, to your friends, to the universe. Words have power. They can heal and they can create. Let your words create the life that you want.

Classic (New-Mom) Smoky Eye

A smoky eye is guaranteed to make a woman feel sexy, whether she's wearing sweatpants and a T or an LBD. It's much easier than you think. We used a plum shade in this illustration, but you can use any color family.

1. Put eye shadow base all over your lids. This will keep your shadow bulletproof and the color fierce all day (or night).

2. Apply a light shimmery shadow all over lid.

3. With a blending brush, sweep a medium shade of shadow in your chosen color family in a windshield-wiper motion from lash line to crease.

4. Dip a crease brush into a darker shade in the same color family and lay the shadow right into the crease of your eye. Don't be afraid to build the color. Blend, blend, blend—you don't want any harsh lines.

5. Use a black pencil to line the upper lashes, getting the color right into the lashes. I like to line the bottom lashes with a color in the same family as the eye shadow colors.

6. Using the crease color and a smudger brush, brush shadow over the top and bottom liner.

7. For the *fiercest* smoky eye, line the inner rim of the lower lashes with black liner, from outer all the way to the inner corner.

8. Finish with two coats of black mascara on the top lashes and one coat on the bottom.

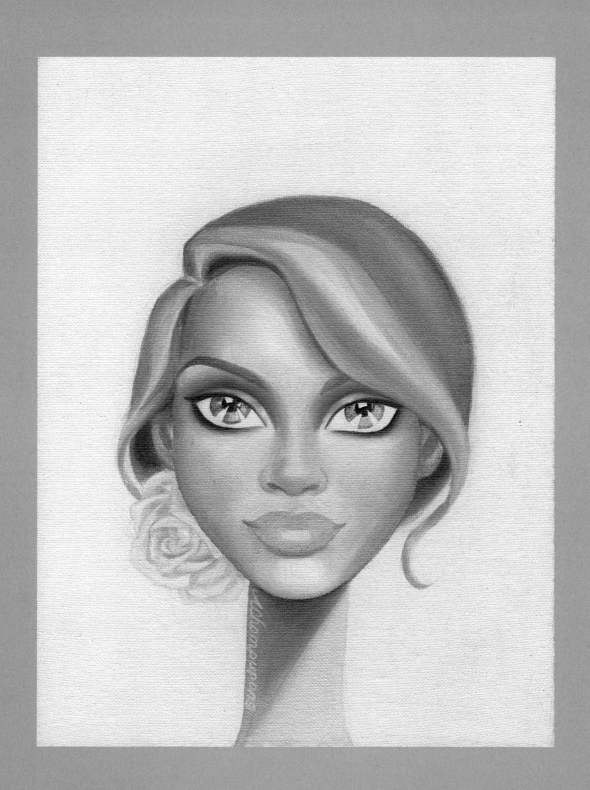

How to Look Like You Got Eight Hours of Sleep When You Really Got Four

It takes way more than concealer to fake a good night's sleep. When you're sleep-deprived, everything looks as if it's sagging a little. All the techniques and tricks I'll show you here will help you look lifted and refreshed.

1. Apply concealer under your eyes, on the inner and outer corners. Blend.

2. Put on foundation to even your skin tone.

3. Add a soft highlighter on cheekbones and inner corners of eyes.

4. Apply pink or peach blush on the apples of your cheeks.

5. Light shimmery shadow goes on lids from lash line to brow.

6. Brush up brows with brow gel. This is key, ladies!

7. A sheer blue-pink lip gloss on lips will brighten your smile.

TICK, TOCK

Ladies, you all know what it's like to keep a million balls in the air. To keep them from crashing down on me, I use minute-by-minute itineraries so everyone knows where they need to be, when, and what they need to do. (I don't believe in information on a need-to-know basis; I need to know *everything*.) It makes me feel secure, and I can see how I'm using my time. Here's a sample of a few of my (more hectic!) days.

MALLY BEAUTY ITINERARY

DAY 1

9:00 A.M.—Mally and team have morning meeting to review all products and sells for the evening show.

10:00 A.M—Mally writes sells for the two new products that still need sells.

11:30 A.M—Mally and Gabrielle revise and finalize the run of show.

12:30–1:00 P.M.—Break for lunch.

1:00 P.M.—Conference call with *Allure* magazine.

1:30–3:00 P.M.—Finalize wardrobe, shoes, and jewelry selections.

3:00 P.M.—Mally departs to pick up the Beans from school.

3:30–5:00 P.M.—Mally spends this time helping the Beans with their homework and play.

5:00 P.M.—Mally departs to QVC for 10:00 P.M. show prep.

5:30 P.M.—Mally's team arrives at QVC for show prep.

6:00 P.M.—Mally arrives at QVC.

6:00 P.M.—Models arrive before shots are taken (17 models for the 10:00 P.M.–12:00 A.M. show).

6:15 P.M.—Models in makeup, Mally in hair and makeup.

7:00 P.M.—Gabrielle meets with the producer to review details for show.

8:00 P.M.—Mally meets with the show's host to review products and their sells.

9:00 P.M.—Models see Mally for approval and touch-ups.

10:00 P.M.–12:00 A.M.—ON THE AIR.

12:00 A.M.—Mally and team depart for NYC.

2:00 A.M.—Mally and team arrive in NYC.

DAY 2

6:00 A.M.—Gabrielle meets Mally to pack and depart for the *Today* show.

6:15 A.M.—Mally and Gabrielle depart for the *Today* show.

6:30 A.M.—Mally and team arrive to meet Jackie Sands at the *Today* show.

6:35 A.M.—Mally in hair and makeup.

7:00 A.M.—Mally reviews talking points for her segment in the 8:00 A.M. hour.

7:30 A.M.—Mally meets with producers for rehearsal.

8:15 A.M.—MALLY LIVE ON THE AIR.

8:30 A.M.—Mally and Gabrielle depart for board meeting; rest of team goes home.

9:00 A.M.–12:00 P.M.—Mally arrives at boardroom in NYC for a board meeting.

12:00 P.M.—Mally departs from the meeting to head to lunch with *InStyle* magazine.

12:30 P.M.—Mally arrives at the restaurant to be interviewed.

2:00 P.M.—Mally departs from lunch and heads to Dr. Ramsey's office to have her teeth cleaned.

2:30 P.M.—Mally's dentist appointment.

4:00 P.M.—Mally departs from dentist and heads to Henri Bendel.

5:00–7:00 P.M.—Mally's personal appearance at Bendel's.

6:30 P.M.—Gabrielle to pick up dinner to eat in the car.

7:00 P.M.—Depart from NYC.

9:30 P.M.—Mally arrives at home! ☺

DAY 3

8:00 A.M.—Mally takes the Beans to school.

9:00 A.M.—Morning meeting with Mally and team.

9:45–10:45 A.M.—Mally and Gabrielle ballet barre class.

11:00–11:30 A.M.—Mally meets the Beans at school for lunch duty and picks Vivienne up.

12:00–12:30 P.M.—Conference call with *People* "StyleWatch" on "Stylish Mommies."

12:30–1:00 P.M.—Lunch with staff.

1:00–2:30 P.M.—Create and plan shot list for upcoming YouTube channel videos.

2:45 P.M.—Mally picks up the Beans at school.

3:30–4:30 P.M.—Mally helps the Beans with homework.

4:30–5:00 P.M.—Review copy for *Redbook* and Glam.com.

5:00–6:00 P.M.—Pick shades for upcoming QVC products (new lip-sticks and shadow sticks for Spring 2015).

6:00 P.M.—Dinner with Phil and the girls.

7:00 P.M.—Bath time.

8:00 P.M.—Bedtime for the girls.

11:00 P.M.—Bedtime for Mally and Phil.

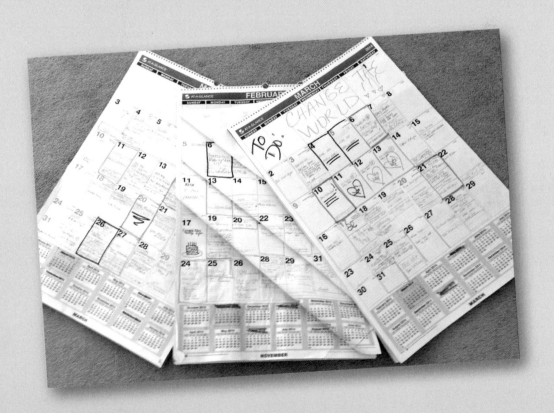

You have my
whole heart
for my whole
life.

chapter

17

Get Your Game Face On

PHIL AND I TEND TO BE A *LITTLE* BIT PROTECTIVE (OKAY, MAYBE a little bit *over*protective) when it comes to our babies. So imagine my shock when one day I noticed that Sophie had a bull's-eye rash on the upper left-hand side of her chest, the kind that screams "Lyme disease!" We live in the country and the girls play outside every day, so tick checks are part of our daily routine. How could we have possibly missed this? We took her to the doctor, who assured us it was just a rash and nothing to worry about. But worry I did, and after a few days, even though she didn't have any other symptoms, I couldn't take it anymore and insisted that the doctor see Sophie again and test her for Lyme.

I had a QVC show that morning, so Phil took Sophie to her appointment. (Double mom guilt: I missed finding that tick AND I couldn't be at her doctor's appointment!) About ten minutes before I had to go on the air, my phone rang. It was Phil. I crossed my fingers and hoped he was going to tell me that Sophie was fine. Instead, he said, "Okay, now, don't freak out. She has Lyme disease."

I immediately burst into tears. I was officially the worst mother in the world. My poor baby! I knew that once Sophie started taking her medicine she'd be okay and that Phil would take good care of her until I got home, but that didn't help me at all. I knew that if I were *really* a good mommy, I would be there with her. Then there was a knock on my door. "Mally! It's time to get miked. Your show's about to begin."

> **"Be as present and committed in your job, no matter what it is, as you are when you're with your family."**

I looked in the mirror. My eyes were red and my nose was running. Well, thank goodness for bulletproof makeup! But you certainly could see that I had been crying. How could I possibly do a two-hour-long live QVC show when my poor child was sick? But something inside me clicked. I realized that I couldn't be there, so I had to be *here*. And the first thing I had to tackle was my red eyes. I pulled out my secret weapons: blue eyeliner and my Lightwand Eye Brightener. I lined my inner rims with the blue, which immediately made my whites look whiter, and used the Lightwand to add brightness to the inner corners of my eyes. Then I took a deep breath through my tears and told myself: "You've got to fake it till you make it! You can get through these two hours, and then you can fall apart. Now you have to give it all you have to make this show count."

I walked onto the set, said a prayer, and offered my show up to Sophie. I told myself I was going to make her proud the same way she always makes me proud. And because I wanted to make the most of that moment so I could get back home to my baby, I came in with so much power and so much strength, and I was so focused on getting my message across and making the models' makeup exquisite, that we sold out of almost every product. It was a win!

Listen: I know you have days when you can't even get out of bed. I know that there are times when you feel weak, scared, like you just can't do it. I know because there have been many times in my life when I felt the same way.

I *know* how hard it is to be a working mom. When I have to leave my babies, it hurts. So what I do, and what you need to do, is make that time away worth the pain. Be as present and committed in your job, no matter what it is, as you are when you're with your family. When you go back to them, your time together will be even sweeter.

When you're faced with a challenge that seems undoable, I want you to take a deep breath. Tell yourself: I can do it. I can do *anything* for ten minutes, an hour, a day. Prove the doubters wrong. Show them that you are tough. No one but you needs to know how you feel inside. Don't forget that putting on your face and looking as if you feel invincible *helps*! That's why I love makeup on days like this; I think of it as my suit of armor. So put on that concealer and that lipstick—it's powerful stuff.

Then if you need to fall apart afterward, do it. If you need to go home and cry in the shower, fine. If you need to go home and climb into bed and feel sorry for yourself, that's okay too, but just get through what you have to get through and *make it count*. Do it and get through it.

You, but Better

We all know that God made you perfect, just the way you are. But He also created makeup so we could play with our look. Want to make your lips appear fuller? Your nose smaller? You'd be *amazed* how many women ask me for these tricks.

How to Make Your Lips Look Fuller

Be careful with this. You want to look natural, not like you OD'd on filler.

1. Exfoliate your lips to get rid of any dry, flaky skin.

2. Apply lip balm and let it sink in for a few minutes, then blot off any excess.

3. Take a lip liner that matches your lip tone or is just a shade deeper. (It shouldn't be sharp; you want a puffy, soft line.) Line your lips, drawing just outside your natural lip line. Rather than accentuating your Cupid's bow, draw a straight line from point to point. You can fill in your lips with the lip liner if you want.

4. Apply a light pink, peach, rose, or nude lipstick or lip gloss all over.

5. Now go, "Mma mma mma!"

6. Put a dab of shimmery lip gloss in the center of your top and bottom lip.

How to Make Your Nose Look Smaller or Narrower

1. Dip a crease brush in a shading powder (don't use bronzer or brown or taupe eye shadow—they have too much pigment) and tap off any excess color.

2. Start where your eyebrow meets the bridge of your nose and apply the powder down both sides of your nose to the tip. The closer the lines are, the narrower your nose will look. (Here's a secret: I admit that sometimes I just tap my two middle fingers into the shading powder, tap them together to remove the excess, and swipe them down the sides of my nose!)

3. Apply the shading color underneath the tip of the nose.

4. Brush a highlighting powder or light concealer down the center of your nose. Hit the tip and put a little between your brows too.

5. Now blend, blend, blend with a clean brush.

Everyday Work Face

Even when things are crazy busy—especially during the workweek—you need to know how to create that perfect everyday face. You know, something that you can put on and look professional in even when you're half asleep and haven't had your first cup of coffee. It's like armor: It makes you invincible.

1. Do your complexion as usual.

2. Start with an eye shadow base all over your eyelids. This will keep everything from traveling.

3. Apply a light, shimmery eye shadow all over, lash line to brow.

4. Use a medium-toned shimmer taupe shadow all over lid, from lash line to crease and under the bottom lash line.

5. Take a deep-taupe matte shade and line your upper lash line. Be sure to bury the shadow deep within the lashes.

6. Take dark-gray eyeliner and, with a very thin line, line the upper lash line.

7. Add two coats of mascara to the top lashes and one to the bottom.

8. Fill in brows. (See page 190.)

9. Add a little soft highlighter on the cheekbones.

10. Use a pinky blush on apples of the cheeks.

11. Finish with a light-rose lip gloss.

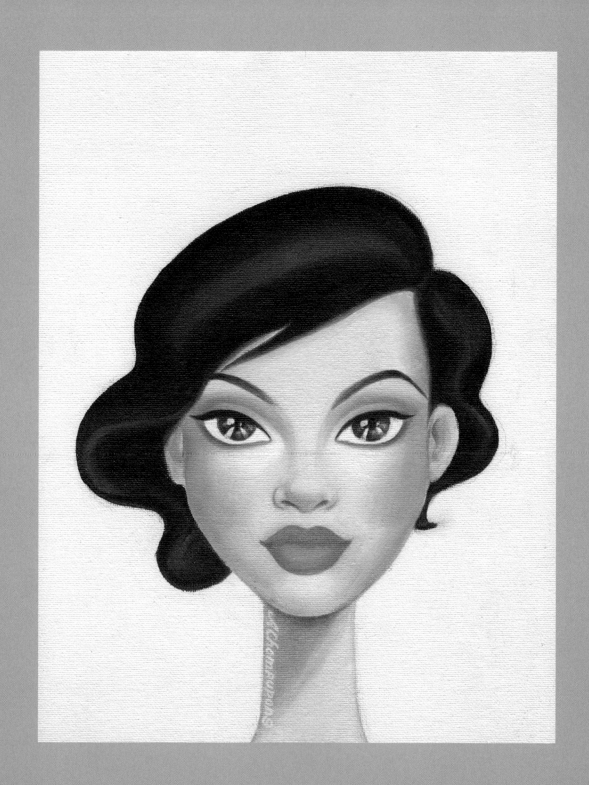

chapter

18

Put on Your Own Oxygen Mask First

I T WAS A TYPICAL MORNING IN THE RONCAL-BICKETT HOUSEHOLD: We had to get three little girls up and dressed, their long hair brushed and braided (my job), and feed them and make their lunches (Phil's job). Then we had to make sure those lunches and their homework and signed permission slips were in their backpacks before they headed out to school. (We prepare for our morning rush the way I prepare for a celebrity photo shoot!) Our dog, Bantay, had to be fed and let out, let back in, and let out again. I had a full day of meetings and phone calls in front of me and a scary-long to-do list. As I stood in front of the bathroom mirror getting ready for the day, I noticed a blemish—okay, a zit—in my hairline. I tried to leave it alone.

About a week later, as I got out of the shower I noticed there was no hair on the place in my hairline where the pimple had been. But I figured it would grow back.

Weeks passed. I showed my little bald spot to everyone. "Isn't this weird?" I'd ask. My friends would agree, then chalk it up to hormones and tell me to forget about it.

Then one day I showed it to my friend Steffanie Attenberg, the publisher of

NewBeauty magazine and a font of knowledge on all things hair-, skin-, and beauty-related.

"What *is* that? Have you gone to a doctor?" she asked. "Honey, you better have that checked out. Do you know what alopecia is?"

My heart sank. "Isn't that when you go bald? When your hair starts to fall out *everywhere*?"

"Yes. I had it when I was a little girl. You should probably call a doctor."

The next morning I woke up and called every dermatologist I knew. I called New York City doctors, Philadelphia doctors, Upstate New York doctors.

A top dermatologist friend was the first to call me back. "Send me a picture," he said. "I want to see what this looks like."

I took an iPhone shot of my bald spot and texted it over to him, and he called me right back. "This looks like alopecia."

My brain started to go a thousand miles a minute. Was I going to go completely bald? What about my eyebrows? What about my eyelashes? My friend assured me that this was not the end of the world. He told me to come see him and we would talk about treatment.

What the hell was I going to do? My hair was my crowning glory, thick and healthy. People always complimented me on it. They assumed I used extensions; I never did. Why was this happening? To *me*? How could I talk about beauty when I didn't feel beautiful myself? That day began a journey for me that I would have never dreamed I would take.

I quickly developed cyberchondria. You know you've had it. It's when you can't stop Googling your symptoms. Search "alopecia" and see what you get. No one really knows why people get it. Stress? Autoimmune disease? Genetics? So many theories, so many opinions, and no answers. The only thing the doctors and scientists know is that there is no cure, and the traditional treatments don't work on everyone. Sometimes your hair grows back, and sometimes it doesn't. Great.

I watched that spot like a hawk. I did everything to make that hair grow: prayer, positive thinking, cortisone shots, yoga, meditation, vitamins, supplements, light therapy, acupuncture. I started mainlining kale and walnuts. I even got a supply of what the Chinese call a "seven-point star," which is basically a small hammer with seven tiny nails embedded in it. Phil "tapped" my spot twice a day, every day, trying to bring energy to the area. When I had to do a public appearance or go on TV, I'd put dark-brown eyeliner or eye shadow on the spot to make it look as if there was hair.

But even with all this attention and action, my hair continued to fall out, and the bald area kept getting bigger and bigger. Even worse, another "satellite" spot appeared in the crown of my head, and that sucker grew like wildfire. At one point, the entire crown of my head was almost completely bald. Oh, and one more thing. A side effect of the cortisone injections was indentations in my scalp. So now I had big bare spots in my hair and a long indentation going down the center of my forehead. It was getting *really* scary.

I cried many tears, especially at night. These kinds of things happened to other people, not to me. I knew that it was nothing that I could control, but I was still so ashamed. And then I felt guilty for feeling sad and sorry for myself! How dare I be sad when it was just hair? There were people in the world who were suffering through much more! So I was ashamed for feeling ashamed. I'm convinced this is something that happens only to women.

> **"I knew that it was nothing that I could control, but I was still so ashamed."**

Phil was always very positive. He kept assuring me that even if I went completely bald, he'd still love me exactly the same way and still think that I was the most beautiful woman in the world. That helped—a little.

As I write this, things aren't back to normal just yet. It turns out that I'm going through the hormone storms and heavy, irregular periods of perimenopause, and that's been affecting my hair and skin. And all the blow-drying and curling irons and styling and pulling on my hair with round brushes traumatized those poor little follicles. I'm still getting cortisone shots once a month. I met with an alo-

With Chuckie Amos, my longtime friend and one of the most talented hair stylists on the planet

pecia specialist, who checked my iron and said that even though my numbers are within the right range, they're on the low side, so why not take some supplements, which I do religiously (no matter how nasty they taste). I get acupuncture and massages. And you know what? (I'm knocking on wood as I type this.) My hair is growing back. Slowly but surely, those little follicles are fighting their way back to health.

But most important, I learned that God sometimes has to yell to get your attention. When I look back on my lifestyle, I lived an athlete's schedule without enough sleep, the proper nutrition, or drinking enough water. I abused my hair and just lived with my crazy, irregular periods. As a wife, mommy, and businesswoman, I took care of everyone but myself. You know when you're on the plane and the flight attendant tells you to put on your own oxygen mask before you help someone else? Just like so many of you, I knew that's what I should do but I didn't do it. Now I know I need to take care of me first so I can take care of others. And I do. (Well, most of the time.)

BECAUSE MY MOM DIED of breast cancer, I've been super-aware and diligent about checkups—I had my first mammogram when I was seventeen, and I never skip a year. I've always had dense and lumpy boobs, and it's totally normal for me to hear the mammogram tech say, "Sorry, but I can't get a good picture. You're going to need an MRI." And I'd have the MRI and get a clean bill of health.

My ob-gyn wanted me to see a breast specialist because of my family history and referred me to one of the best breast specialists in the country. Phil accompanied me. During the manual exam, the doctor stopped on the spot that always got an eyebrow raise out of every one of my doctors and said, "I'm going to do a little ultrasound."

It wasn't my first, and there had never been a problem before, so I wasn't too worried. The doctor squeezed warm gel over my breast and moved the transducer around while she looked at the screen. She hit the PRINT button, ripped off the paper, and said, "I'll be right back."

In a few minutes the doctor returned. "I don't want you to be alarmed, but I think it's a good idea if we biopsy that breast," she said.

> **"I had my first mammogram when I was seventeen, and I never skip a year."**

I was scheduled for an MRI-guided biopsy; between the hospital's schedule and the doctor's schedule and my schedule, we couldn't get it done right away. It was an exercise in not worrying, which is something I'm not very good at.

When the day for the procedure finally came, I was a lot more nervous than I thought I would be. The amazing nurses and doctors at the hospital tried to make me feel as comfortable as possible, but let's just say that the experience wasn't a run through Bergdorf's.

I had the procedure on a Thursday; I was leaving on Friday night for an appearance on QVC U.K. We were told I had to wait forty-eight hours for the results of the biopsy, so I wouldn't hear from the doctor until I returned home on Monday. I was still in pain from the procedure (and wrapped up in an ACE bandage), but I knew I had to focus on the job ahead, no matter how anxious I was.

Friday evening I was giving the girls their baths before the car came to take me to the airport. My cell phone buzzed, but I had my hands full of wet children and got to it just in time to register that the number showing on the phone was that of my doctor's office. The first thought I had was that she was calling to tell me I had breast cancer.

Phil helped me get the girls out of the tub and I called the doctor back—only to get a message saying the office was closed. I called the answering service and left a message that I was getting on a plane and *had* to speak to the doctor before I left, then called my doctor again and got the same "the office is closed" message. I called again and again. I was getting ready to leave when my phone rang and I saw my doctor's number.

Phil and I went into my office; he sat with his hands in prayer, eyes closed, as I answered the phone.

"Dr. Y? I'm sorry I missed your call."

"Mally," she said, and paused. I could almost hear her smile through the phone as she said my name. "I love making these phone calls."

I looked at Phil and mouthed, "*YES!* I'm okay!"

When I got off the phone, we both burst into happy tears and fell to our knees in gratitude to say a prayer of thanks.

If someone in your immediate family has, or has had, any kind of cancer, you know that the C word does not discriminate, and there's always the worry *Do I have it too? Will it get me?* hanging over your head. My loves, this is my plea to you: Go for your physicals and checkups to make sure you are healthy. Do your manual exams. Get your mammograms regularly. I always feel that there are two kinds of people: those who get a little worrywart-ish and go to the doctor for a paper cut, and others who are afraid to know, so they ignore it and push it away. Please, put yourself first and find out. Prevention is the best medicine. We need you.

The Feel-Good Face

We all have days when we wake up and feel like shit, but staying in bed is not an option. Let me show you how to look great when you feel anything but. This look is all about lightness, brightness, and lifting your face *and* your spirits.

1. Apply foundation and spot-conceal any blemishes, redness around your nose, or dark circles.

2. Sweep a bone-colored shadow with a hint of shimmer from lash line to brow.

3. Using shimmery brown shadow, contour the eyelid crease and apply under the lower lashes.

4. Line your eyes using the natural-liner technique (page 48) with dark brown or black, or try navy or dark green for a pop of color.

5. Fill in your brows; that will give your face an instant lift.

6. Use two coats of mascara on the top lashes and one on the bottom.

7. Use highlighter on your cheekbones and a peachy blush on the apples of your cheeks, blended up to the cheekbones.

8. Add a peachy lip gloss for a natural glow.

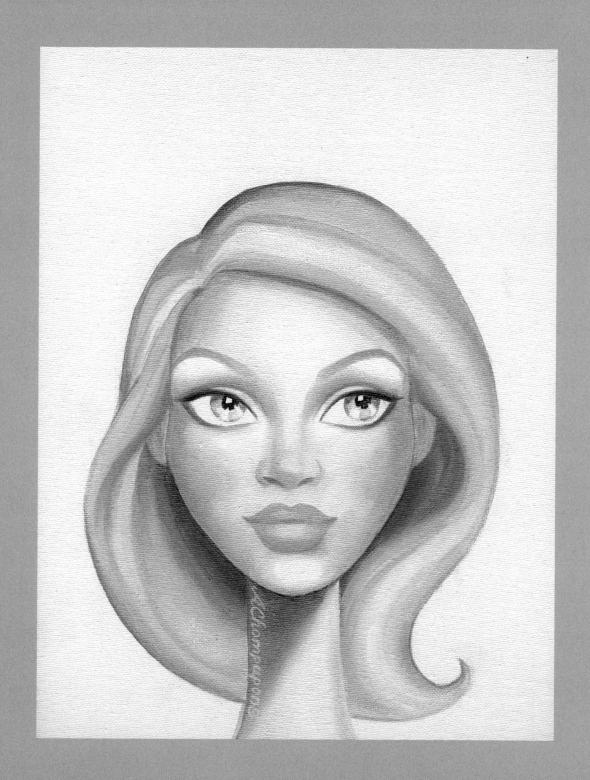

chapter

19

Your Most Gorgois Days Are Ahead of You

O KAY, MY LOVES, I'M GOING to get on my soapbox now.

Why do so many beautiful women believe that as they get older they become less attractive? Nothing makes me madder than a woman saying, "Oh, I used to be beautiful in my twenties [or thirties or forties], but now it's all over. It's downhill from here."

Getting older is inevitable, but it doesn't mean we should give up on taking care of ourselves—*au contraire!* Think of each new phase in your life as a time of discovery: Take that yoga class, schedule that massage and facial, try that new moisturizer. When I was in my twenties, I never went to

the gym: Dancing all night at the clubs was all the exercise I needed. Today I swear by my ballet barre class and Pilates; I have muscles and definition in my arms that I never had before, and I love it.

My new mantra is "Healthy is the new young." I'm not talking about just having a strong, healthy body but about having the attitude to go with it. It's a lot of work keeping up with all those PYTs (Pretty Young Things)—believe me, I work in the beauty industry and I know. But is that the way you want to spend your time? Once I decided to embrace my age, it was so liberating! I don't mean that I stopped trying and let things slide (in more ways than one!), but I realized that young does not equal beautiful. All the Botox and fillers in the world can't make you look better if you have dull, dry skin or if your teeth are yellow and your eyes bloodshot. (In fact, teeth whitening and eyedrops are two of the easiest ways to wake up your face and freshen your look.)

"Healthy is the new young."

I've found that as women get older, they often cling to makeup colors and textures that they wore when they were in their teens and twenties, or they give up on it altogether. If you're still wearing the face you put on ten or twenty years ago, I hate to break it to you, but it's making you look older, not more youthful. (Of course, there are exceptions to every rule. Style icons like Vivienne Westwood, Patricia Field, and Betsey Johnson, all in their seventies, totally own the unique and extreme style and makeup looks they wear. As Oribe once said in an interview with *W* magazine: "When you get to a certain age, you gotta go gangster.")

But for most of us, our makeup should change as we do. It's not about slavishly following trends but about what flatters us and suits our lives. When we were younger, we welcomed change; why not do that now?

I've always been a girl's girl, and I always will be. My adventure with Mommy at Saks aside, when I was in junior high school and we weren't allowed to wear makeup to school, my goal was to look as if I wasn't wearing makeup at all (except maybe for that blue eyeliner). In high school and college and into my twenties, I had no fear—there was no such thing as too much! As a young makeup artist, I was on top of the latest trends; I would give any hot look a shot, whether it suited me or not. Look—I even shaved my eyebrows so I could draw them on where I thought they should be. (Also: platinum-blond hair; airbrushed nails.)

On my wedding day, everyone expected me to walk down the aisle with smoky eyes and a dramatic, theatrical look, but I appeared with softer and more-natural makeup in shades of taupe and pink. It reflected the emotional and mental transformation I was going through and the new persona I was excited to explore. Looking back, I also think I was subconsciously retraining my eye; I knew that when we had kids I'd need to be more comfortable with a look that didn't take a lot of time.

And I was right. Instead of getting up at 2:00 A.M. to put on a face for an early photo-shoot call, I was getting up for 2:00 A.M. feedings. I barely had time to put on lip gloss, so I had to be inventive. I figured out the products and techniques that would create the most impact in the least time. Now that the girls are a bit older, they sit with me—just like I sat with my mom—while I put on my makeup, and I have a little more time to work on that smoky eye while I spend time with them.

With some help from me, you can and will be the most gorgois you have ever been. You may need to stretch, to try new things and be willing to break some old habits. Are you ready? Maybe you've been wearing the same makeup look for the last fifteen years. Maybe you're stuck in a bit of a rut with your skin-care or color choices. No worries, it happens to all of us (yes, even me!). *You gotta wake up your makeup!* Maybe a bold lip color is destined to be your new signature. Maybe it's time for a new haircut and color. All it takes is some inspiration, time, and an open mind. Think of me as your little Filipina cheerleader, standing on the sidelines. You can do it. And, hey, it's only makeup. If you don't like it, you can always wash it off.

I can't say it enough: Your age has nothing to do with your beauty, my loves. Coco Chanel said that nature gives you the face you have at twenty, but the face you have at fifty is the one you deserve. Those "crow's feet" around your eyes? They mean you've smiled—a lot! Be the kick-ass older woman younger women aspire to be—confident, generous, strong. I can show you how to create a flawless complexion, long and lush lashes, and a plush pout, but it's your spirit, your experience, and your inner fire that truly make you beautiful.

Perfect Natural Brow

Eventually, the brow-plucking we did over the years starts to catch up with us. Add to that the thinning and lightening (or graying) of the hairs that happen naturally as we get older, and some of us barely have anything left at all. Across the board, as you get older, a fuller, well-groomed brow is the way to go. Here's my go-to method.

Note: Your eyebrows are not identical twins; they're more like sisters. (In my case, they're barely distant cousins!) It's kind of like your boobs; it's okay that they're not the same. Learning the right way to enhance your brows can lift your whole face.

1. Take a brow pencil and lay it alongside your nose so it touches the inner corner of your eye. Mark the spot with your pencil; this is where your brow should begin. Now line up the pencil with the outer corner of your iris (the colored part of your eye). This is highest part of the arch. Finally, take your pencil from the edge of your nose to the outside corner of your eye; this is where your eyebrow should end.

2. Now: Take a brow spoolie and comb up your brows.

3. Take a very sharp brow pencil one shade lighter than your brows (one shade darker than your brows if you're blonde).

4. Set your brows with a shadow in the same shade as the pencil to make them truly bulletproof and to soften.

5. Brush brow gel up through your brows to set them and seal in the color.

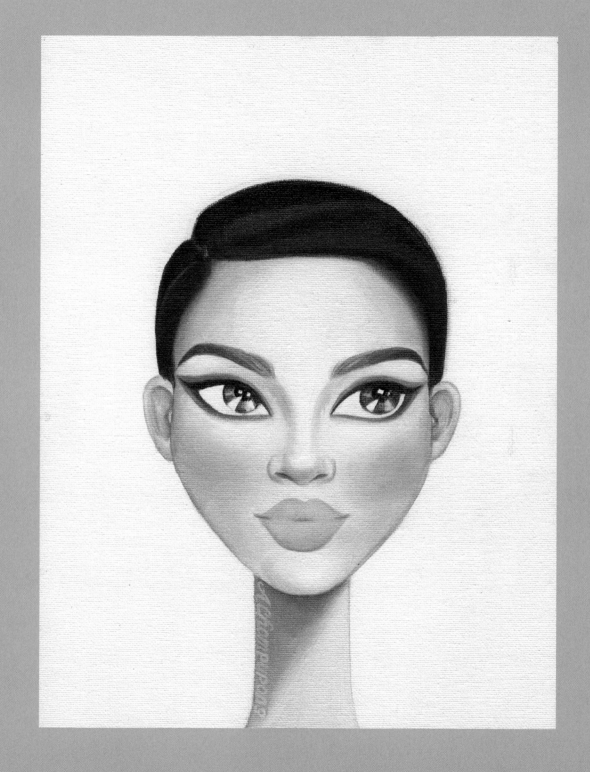

The I'm-Not-21-Anymore (and-That's-Okay!) Face

As we age, there are certain little tricks that we all should know. When it comes to a mature woman, it's all about opening up the eyes, brightening and bringing color back to the skin, and juicifying those lips. I love it when an older woman takes the time to embrace how beautiful she is and goes there with some color.

1. Create your perfect complexion (see page 18). Use creamy moisturizing products, and remember—no translucent powder! It settles into fine lines and ages you.

2. Put on a soft smoky eye (see page 158) using nude or gray shadow, working it into the crease for definition.

3. Line the upper lashes with a dark gray or soft black pencil.

4. Use two coats of mascara on the top lashes, one on the bottom.

5. Now add some color: Apply pink blush on the apples of your cheeks, blending it up toward your temples.

6. Put on a bright-pink lipstick or gloss, or another color with a pop. A blue pink is always a good option; it not only brightens the lips and the face but also makes your teeth look whiter. Which *never* gets old.

chapter

20

Gratitude Rules My Life

CAN'T BEGIN TO COUNT THE THINGS I HAVE TO BE GRATEFUL FOR. I don't take anything for granted. I'm constantly saying thank you. I'm the dork who says, "Thank you for this amazing chandelier, dear Lord." I say thank you when I can zip up my skinny jeans without having to lie down on the floor. I say thank you when I hear my baby girl singing a Disney song in the bathroom. I say thank you when a woman comes up to me in the pharmacy and tells me that my mascara has changed her life. I say thank you when that car that ran the red light just misses my passenger-side door. I say thank you when my Filipino chicken adobo turns out exactly like my stepmother's.

My father taught me to say thank you as soon as I open my eyes in the morning. I love this ritual, because it really does set your mind in the right place. You have another day to make good, fix your mistakes, and conquer the world. My dad taught me another cool ritual: When I get out of bed, I put my right foot down on the rug and say "thank," then I put my left foot down and say "you." Of course, I take everything to the extreme and say "thank" (right foot), "you" (left foot), all the way to the bathroom.

I even say thank you for the crappy things, like missing a train or getting to work and realizing you left your lunch on the counter, because I believe these things happen for a reason.

I even believe my mother's death, and all the pain and suffering that losing her caused me, has a purpose. I believe that I am meant to honor her legacy not only with my life but also by connecting with other motherless and fatherless people to help heal our wounds of loss. Breast cancer awareness is also a cause new and dear to my heart. I do what I can to support these women, from giving hugs to creating a "Your Best Days Are Ahead" kit; it's sold on QVC in their honor, and I donate a portion of the profits to research to help rid our world of cancer. (I know, it's a bold statement, but you've learned by now that I like to say things out loud to make them come to pass!)

mallybeauty   20w

442 likes

mallybeauty Say it with me, Mallynistas: "My Brightest Days are Ahead!!!!" Thanks to your love and support, we've raised $33,000 for #BreastCancer research!! THANK YOU!!!

SAY THANK YOU

We say grace before every meal; we even say grace for Bantay and Pandy, our rescue dogs: *Dear Lord, thank you for the gift of these dogs. Please bless them, make them happy and healthy; make them the best dogs ever and please help Pandy so she stops jumping on the table. Please bless the Barbie that Bantay ate and let it come out safely. In Jesus's name; amen.*

Keep on truckin'!

And don't you know that they wait until we've finished saying grace and we say, "Eat!" before they eat?

Phil and I pray with the girls every night before they go to bed. We always start with a thank-you: for our blessings, for our gifts, for the opportunities God has given us, for every single great thing and bad thing in our lives, because they all mean something. We say thank you for everyone in the family and ask blessings on our friends and family, wherever they are. We ask for health in body, mind, and spirit, joy, peace, understanding, and protection and that our hearts be open to all good things. We ask God to guide our steps and to watch over us all.

Then Phil and I say our prayers before we go to bed. Phil's very focused, but emotional. I go on for a while; I like specifics, and my list gets very long. Sometimes he's asleep before I'm finished, and I have to poke him in the ribs for the "amen."

WITH GRATITUDE COME BLESSINGS, and with those blessings the responsibility to give to others. I'm a huge lover of random acts of kindness. Pay for coffee for the person in line behind you. Compliment a stranger. Give a homeless man your to-go box. Babysit for a single mother. Donate blood. Put a quarter in a meter that's about to run out. Spend time with a senior citizen who lives alone. Praise your coworkers or assistants when they do something great. Just typing these things makes my heart flutter.

Like my mother, I believe we were put on this earth to take care of and inspire one another. No matter what way or who it is, you come into contact with a person because you were supposed to. Whether it's your husband or a friend or a neighbor or a homeless man, that person was put in front of you for a reason. I believe deep, deep down that there's a reason for everything, even for things that seem unbearable at the time.

Before I go, I want to thank you: Thank you for spending some of your precious time with me. Thank you for opening your mind, heart, and soul to some of my thoughts, techniques, and ideas. It humbles me so much to be in your life, even in the smallest way. Thank you for blessing this world with your own unique perfection. I want you to know that you are loved, cherished, adored, and appreciated. I am grateful for you and I want you to be grateful for you, too! Now, one tiny request before I sign off: Look in the mirror and say thank you for that fierce, fearless, joyful, gorgois creature that you see there! If you can, please also do that with a smile, a butt wiggle, and two snaps in the air. Then my work here is really done!

Love you and God bless,
Mally

Acknowledgments

Thank you Lord, for all my blessings. I am not worthy of all the gifts You have given me. To God be the Glory!

My Mally Beauty Team: Thank you for sharing your love, passion, talents with me. I appreciate and cherish you all every single day.

To my family at BP Packaging, I love you and thank you!

Jim Indorato, thank you for being that one person. You mean the world to me.

To Kalinka and Tracy Reese, thank you for giving me my first jobs and for being strong, talented role models! I love you!

To Charles Chang, the family and friends who believed in us before Mally Beauty was born. Thank you for the faith. All my love.

To Jim Hainis, thank you for such a beautiful cover and for making everything so GORGOIS all these years. Your friendship and work ethic are priceless.

My outstanding teams at Tractenberg and Planit, you blow me away every day. And shoutout to Jackie, Dana, and Erin, who answer all my calls even at the ass-crack of dawn!

To my vendors: You're our family and we can't do this without you.

To all my retail partners: Ulta, Henri Bendel, Beauty.com, Amazon.com, Fred Segal, QVC U.K., QVC Italy, QVC Germany, Birchbox, and the ones who believed first—my beloved QVC U.S. Thank you for allowing me to share my message, educate with my products, and literally invade 100 million households on a regular basis!

To the heart and soul of QVC, who mean so much to me: the backstage crew, operations desk, producers, models, security, and custodial staff. Thank you for all you are. I am honored to know and work with you.

To all the QVC hosts, thank you for the love, laughs, and expertise. Love dancing with you!

To every TV producer and magazine editor that I have ever worked with: Thank you for trusting me!

To Magic Mike, Tim, and everyone shooting video behind the camera. Thank you for making me look as good as possible, for creating moving magic, and for your kind hearts.

Jennie Tung, thank you for your support, love, understanding, and for making that first phone call!

Sydny Miner, thank you for your dedication, organization, and hard work!

All the team at Ballantine, thank you for everything! I am so humbled!

Alisa Chompupong, thank you for the amazing twenty-two-year friendship and beautiful illustrations. Your talent never ceases to amaze me!

To every single makeup artist, hairstylist, photographer, and stylist I have had the honor to work with, thank you for the inspiration.

Chuckaluk and Aggie, thank you for the beginning of the journey! I will never be in a motor home and not think of you!

My Mally Beauty makeup artists, especially Jorge and Masako: Thank you for your talented hands and great hearts!

All my clients and their teams: Thank you for the love and opportunities. I am so very blessed.

To Kate and Say, thanks for all your hard work and dedication. And Say, for all those hours we clocked in the car. Text me when you get home!

To Ernetta, Lisa, Barb, Corinne, Alicia, and anyone who has worked with us to care for our babies. Thank you for your love and kindness.

To my girls, Gabrielle and Chrissy. You are my soldiers! There are no words to say what you mean to me. Thank you for your love, support, dedication, talent, laughter, and heart. No one kicks ass like you!

My friends who have been with me through thick and thin. You know who you are and you will always have my loyalty!

To Teenie: I am so proud of the woman you've become and watching your journey has been so inspiring. You will forever be in my heart. YOU!!!! YOU!!!!!

To Chrissy and Tracey: I'm blessed and honored to be your Ate. Thank you for your love, encouragement, and support my whole life and for never letting me feel alone. I will forever see you walking out into the woods!

To my extended family, all my aunties and uncles and all my cousins, especially the ones I grew up with, Tina, Susie, Philip A, Ray, Markie, Malu, Juni, Voltaire, Reuben, Rocki. I am blessed and honored to be related to you!

Marty and Joe Bickett: Thank you for falling in love and making that man who became my husband. I am so honored to be your daughter-in-law. I love you.

To my Sweet Daddy and my beautiful stepmom: Drs. Rogelio and Fely Roncal. Daddy, through all of these years, we've been through so much. After Mommy died, we only got stronger. You filled me with so much confidence, faith, and belief in myself that no matter what, I knew I could succeed as long as you were by my side. And Fely, you have become such a part of my heart and the most amazing Lola to our daughters. I love you so much.

Thank you, my Mommy. Not a day goes by that I don't hear your laugh or feel your hug. Thank you for shining your light on me. Till we are together again . . .

And to Phil, Pilar, Sophie, and Vivienne. I can't do any of this without you. You have my whole heart for my whole life.

To my Mallynistas: without you, I would not be here. I am humbled to be in your life. God bless you!

Makeup Product Guide

Here's a guide to the Mally Beauty products and colors I used to create the looks in my book. I finish *every* look by applying my Face Defender. It's simply magic. Think of it as the world's first clear "powder"—it mattifies and sets your makeup, creating a flawless finish without changing the color.

Skin Care How-To (page 8)
Lip balm: Perfect Prep Lip System

How to Light Up the Room (page 18)
Primer: Perfect Prep Poreless Primer
Concealer: Cancellation Concealer System
Tinted powder: Poreless Perfection Skin Finisher *or* Poreless Perfection Shaded Skin Finisher
Liquid Foundation: Ultimate Performance Professional Foundation
Powder foundation: Poreless Perfection Foundation

Cream foundation: Ultimate Performance Professional Foundation *or* Face Defender BB Cream Foundation

For a Tween or Young Teen (page 28)
Tinted moisturizer: Face Defender BB Cream Foundation
Concealer: Age Rebel Nourishing Concealer
Sheer lip gloss: High-Shine Liquid Lipstick (in Pearly Girl or Starburst)

For an Older Teen or Early Twentysomething (page 30)

Concealer: Cancellation Concealer System
Lightweight Powder Foundation: Visible Skin Adjustable Coverage Foundation
Peach blush: Blush Singles (in Georgia Peach)
Pink blush: Blush Singles (in Pink Glow)
Light matte or shimmery eye shadow: Effortless Airbrush Nourishing Eyeshadow in Champagne
Light lip gloss: High-Shine Liquid Lipstick (in Mally's Baby)

Natural Eyeliner (page 48)

Top, Evercolor Starlight Waterproof Eyeliner (in Midnight); bottom, Evercolor Starlight Eyeliner (in Milk Chocolate)
Top, Evercolor Starlight Waterproof Eyeliner (in Royal Plum or Dark Chocolate); bottom, Evercolor Starlight Waterproof Eyeliner (in Bronze)
Top, Ultimate Performance Waterproof Eyeliner (in Glide & Go Gray or Navy); bottom, Ultimate Performance Waterproof Eyeliner (in Shimmering Taupe)

Blush (page 50)

24/7 Professional Blush System

Mascara and Concealer (page 60–62)

Mascara: Volumizing Mascara
Concealer: Cancellation Concealer System, Cancellation Conditioning Concealer, Age Rebel Nourishing Concealer, Age Rebel Concealer Stick, or 24/7 Professional Full Coverage Concealer System

2-Minute Face (page 72)

Concealer: Cancellation Concealer System, Cancellation Conditioning Concealer, Age Rebel Nourishing Concealer, Age Rebel Concealer Stick or 24/7 Professional Full Coverage Concealer System
Powder foundation: Poreless Perfection Foundation
Mascara: Volumizing Mascara

5-Minute Face (page 74)

Brows: 24/7 Brow Express
Eyeliner: Evercolor Starlight Waterproof Eyeliner (in Midnight, top; in Milk Chocolate, bottom)
Blush: 24/7 Professional Blush System

10-Minute Face (page 76)

Eyeshadow base: Eye Shadow Base (in Neutral)
Shimmering brown, taupe, or dusky plum eyeshadow: Effortless Airbrush Nourishing Eyeshadow (in Brightening Brown), or Evercolor Shadow Stick (in Taupe or Dusk)
Highlighter: Poreless Face Defender Super Natural Highlighter

My Classic Hollywood Face (page 78)

Foundation: Ultimate Performance Professional Foundation
Highlighter and blush: 24/7 Professional Blush System with Glow (in Pink Satin)
Eye shadow base: Eye Shadow Base
Eye shadow: champagne: City Chick Smokey Eye Kit (Brownstone Highlighter shade); matte taupe: City Chick Smokey Eye Kit (inTribeca Taupe,

lid shade), or Eyelift Shadow Duo (in Taupe, deeper shade)

Black pencil eyeliner: Evercolor Starlight Waterproof Eyeliner Singles (in Midnight)

Black liquid eyeliner: Ultimate Performance Ink Liner *and* Evercolor Lasting Liquid Eyeliner (in Black)

Brows: 24/7 Brow Express *and* Brow Beauty Pencil

Red lipstick: Perfect Red Lip Kit

Man-Friendly Makeup (page 90)

Concealer: Age Rebel Concealer Stick *or* Ultimate Performance Perfector Pencil Duo

Powder foundation: Poreless Perfection Foundation

Gold eye shadow: In the Buff 2 Eyeshadow Palette (Egyptian Gold)

Mascara: Volumizing Mascara

Highlighter: Lightwand Eye Brightener

Soft pink blush: Couture Color Custom Blush (in Bliss or Romance)

Soft pink lip balm: Perfect Prep Lip System

Big-Day Makeup (page 92)

Foundation: Ultimate Performance Full Coverage Liquid Foundation *or* Ultimate Performance Professional Foundation

Light shimmery eye shadow: City Chick Smokey Eye Kit (Brownstone Highlighter shade)

Shimmery brown eye shadow: City Chick Smokey Eye Kit (Brownstone Lid shade)

Dark brown eyeliner: Evercolor Starlight Waterproof Eyeliner (in Espresso)

Pink blush: Blush Singles (in Mally's Glow)

Baby pink lipstick: The Perfois Pink Lip Kit (in Soft Pink)

The I-Mean-Business Face (page 102)

Foundation: Ultimate Performance Full Coverage Liquid Foundation

Highlighter and peachy blush: Shimmer, Shape, and Glow

Eye shadow base, nude and matte brown eye shadow: City Chick Smokey Eye Kit (in Brownstone)

Black eye pencil: Evercolor Starlight Waterproof Eyeliner (in Midnight)

Mascara: Volumizing Mascara

Contour: Shimmer, Shape, and Glow

Nude lipstick and lip gloss: The Perfect Nude Lip Kit

Have Fun with Color (page 110)

Eyeshadow: I Love Color Eyeshadow Palette (Pop Art Blue or Fantasy Green)

Eyeliner: Evercolor Starlight Waterproof Eyeliner (in Peacock Feathers, Caribbean Sea, Deep Violet, Black Cherry, or Ice Blue) *or* Ultimate Performance Waterproof Eyeliner (in Auto Pilot Violet, Blue Streak, or Green Means Go)

Mascara: Volumizing Mascara

Be Sparkly! (Glitter Eye) (page 114)

Luminizer: Finish Line Professional Luminizer

Beyoncé (page 122)

Concealer: Cancellation Conditioning Concealer

Highlight: Believable Bronzer

Shimmery bronzy-brown eye shadow: In the Buff 2 Eyeshadow Palette (Toasted Sugar)

Black eye pencil: Evercolor Starlight Waterproof Eyeliner (in Midnight)

Eye shadow/highlighter: In the Buff 2 Eyeshadow Palette (Whipped Cream)

Mascara: Volumizing Mascara

Blush: Believable Bronzer

Blue-pink lip gloss: High-Shine Liquid Lipstick (in Life Is Fuchsia)

The Sculpted Face (page 132)

Highlighter/shaping powder: Shimmer, Shape, and Glow

Cream: Pro-tricks Correcting Palette

Bright, Beautiful Eyes (page 140)

Eye shadow base: Eye Shadow Base

Eye shadow: champagne shimmer: In the Buff Eyeshadow Palette (Golden Tiger's Eye); matte blonde: In the Buff 2 Eyeshadow Palette (Blonde)

Eyeliner: Evercolor Starlight Waterproof Eyeliner (in Midnight)

Mascara: Volumizing Mascara

Bronzer How-To (page 146)

Bronzer: Believable Bronzer

The Perfect Nude Lip (page 148)

Lipstick, liner, and gloss: The Perfect Nude Lip

Classic (New-Mom) Smoky Eye (page 158)

Eye shadow base, shimmer shadow, dark shadow: City Chick Smokey Eye Kit (in Plum Chelsea)

Black eye pencil: Evercolor Starlight Waterproof Eyeliner (in Midnight)

Mascara: Volumizing Mascara

How to Look Like You Got Eight Hours of Sleep When You Really Got Four (page 160)

Concealer: 24/7 Professional Full Coverage Concealer System

Foundation: Poreless Perfection Foundation, Ultimate Performance Professional Foundation, Face Defender BB Cream Foundation, *or* Visible Skin Adjustable Coverage Foundation

Highlighter: Finish Line Professional Luminizer

Pink blush: Blush Singles (in Pink Glow)

Peach blush: Blush Singles (in Peachy Glow)

Light shimmery shadow: Celebrate! Eye Shadow

Brow gel: Brightening Brow Gel

Blue-pink lip gloss: High-Shine Liquid Lipstick in Must Have Pink

How to Make Your Lips Look Fuller (page 172)

Exfoliator and lip balm: Perfect Prep Lip System

Lip liner: The Perfect Nude Lip

Pink, peach, rose, nude lipstick: High-Shine Liquid Lipstick (in Mally's Baby, Fuzzy Navel, Delish, or Natural Nude)

Shimmery lip gloss: High-Shine Liquid Lipstick (in Pearly Girl)

How to Make Your Nose Look Smaller or Narrower (page 173)

Shaping and highlighting powders: Shimmer, Shape, and Glow

Everyday Work Face (page 174)

Eye shadow base: Eye Shadow Base

Light shimmery shadow: City Chick Smokey Eye Kit (Canal Street Khaki Highlighter shade)

Medium-toned taupe shimmer shadow: In the Buff Eyeshadow Palette (Shimmering Taupe)

Deep taupe matte shadow: City Chick Smokey Eye Kit (Canal Street Khaki Crease shade)

Dark gray eyeliner: Evercolor Starlight Waterproof Eyeliner (in Gunmetal)

Mascara: Volumizing Mascara

Brows: Brow Beauty Ultimate Brow Kit

Highlighter: Finish Line Professional Luminizer or Shimmer, Shape, and Glow (Shimmer)

Pink blush: Blush Singles (in Fantasy Blush)

Light rose lip gloss: High-Shine Liquid Lipstick (in Tender Rose)

The Feel-Good Face (page 184)

Foundation: Poreless Perfection Foundation

Concealer: Age Rebel Nourishing Concealer

Bone eye shadow: In the Buff 2 Eyeshadow Palette (French Vanilla)

Shimmery brown shadow: In the Buff 2 Eyeshadow Palette (Oak)

Eyeliner: Evercolor Starlight Waterproof Eyeliner (in Sailor)

Brows: 24/7 Brow Express

Mascara: Volumizing Mascara

Highlighter: Finish Line Professional Luminizer

Peach blush: Liquid Face Defender Blush (in Mimosa)

Peach lip gloss: High-shine Liquid Lipstick (in Perfois Peach)

Perfect Natural Brow (page 190)

Brow pencil and gel: Brow Beauty Ultimate Brow Kit

The I'm-Not-21-Anymore (and-That's-Okay!) Face (page 192)

Primer: Perfect Prep Poreless Primer

Concealer: Cancellation Concealer System

Foundation: Ultimate Performance Professional Foundation

Smoky eye shadow: City Chick Smokey Eye Kit (Tribeca Taupe)

Dark gray or soft black eye pencil: Ultimate Performance Waterproof Eyeliner (in Glide & Go Gray)

Mascara: Volumizing Mascara

Pink blush: Blush Singles (in Plum Pretty)

Bright pink lipstick or gloss: High-Shine Liquid Lipstick (in Lipety Split), The Perfois Pink Lip Kit (in Bright Pink), or The Perfect Bright Lip Kit (in Frisky Fuchsia)

About the Author

Celebrity makeup artist MALLY RONCAL is the founder and president of the Mally Beauty cosmetics line, a QVC star, and a columnist for *Redbook*. The daughter of an ob-gyn mother and a clinical psychiatrist father, Mally planned to study dermatology but ultimately earned a degree in fine art and entered the fashion industry. One of the most sought-after makeup artists in the industry, with a client list that includes such stars as Beyoncé and Celine Dion, she has been featured in *The New York Times*, *People*, *O: The Oprah Magazine*, *Allure*, *InStyle*, *Cosmopolitan*, *Marie Claire*, and *Good Housekeeping* and has appeared on *Today*, *The View*, *Rachael Ray*, *The Wendy Williams Show*, *The Dr. Oz Show*, and *The Oprah Winfrey Show*.

mallybeauty.com
Facebook.com/mallybeauty
YouTube.com/MallyTVProductions
@mallybeauty
Instagram.com/mallybeauty